GW00367803

BALI
AT COST

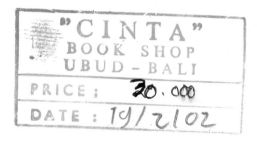

Lynne Maree Smith

Little Hills Press

© Photographs by the Author and Indonesian Tourist Board.
© Maps, Little Hills Press, 1992
©This revised edition, **January 1995**
Cover by IIC
Maps by Angela and Mark Butler
Printed in Australia
© Lynne Smith
Illustrations by Joseph Tabone

ISBN 1 86315 071 4

Little Hills Press Pty Ltd
37-43 Alexander Street
Crows Nest NSW 2065 Australia

Moorland Publishing Company Ltd
Moor Farm Road
Airfield Estate, Ashbourne
Derbyshire DE6 1HD England

DISCLAIMER

While all care has been taken by the publisher and author to ensure that the information is accurate and up to date, the publisher does not take responsibility for the information published herein. The recommendations are those of the author and as things get better or worse, places close down and others open, some elements in the book may be inaccurate when you get there. Please write and tell us about it so we can update in subsequent editions.

Little Hills ^{TM} and are registered trademarks of Little Hills Press Pty Ltd.

ACKNOWLEDGMENTS

Special thanks to Mark Naylor for the surfing section.

A big *terima kasih* to the Bali Government Tourism Offices in Denpasar and Kuta.

And thanks to Mum and Roger for checking the original proofs.

CONTENTS

BALI

AN INTRODUCTION

Bali has been described as the "sanctuary of the gods", the "island of a thousand temples", the "morning of the world" and a tropical paradise. A speck on the world map, it has become the favoured destination for many travellers. An island of contrasts, Bali offers something for everyone: hedonists who desire nothing more than to relax in luxury, sip cocktails and watch the sunset, need look no further; or for the budget traveller, eager to explore the mysteries of an enigmatic island on a shoestring, Bali's the place.

Bali is surrounded by palm-fringed, crystal-clear waters and vibrant coral gardens. White, shimmering sands and pounding surf, or black-crystal beaches and gentle, lapping waves — Bali offers a multitude of watersports. Not far from the coast, hills are meticulously terraced, resembling green stairways to the heavens and majestic volcanoes (the thrones of the gods) loom over the scenery, punctuated by ornate pagodas. The cultivated land, like that created by a landscape gardener, reflects the order and elegance of its people.

Bali's culture is unique and paradoxical. In one sense, the traditional Hindu culture has been preserved intact, despite Western "invasions" and the predominance of Islam in the archipelago. In another sense, the culture is dynamic, and the people, forever curious, welcome new ideas. Bali isn't a fossilised relic, it is alive and well, and for this the gods should be thanked. For essentially, it is the people's pleasure in satisfying the gods that fosters the Hindu culture and adds to the visitor's fascination with the island.

INDONESIA

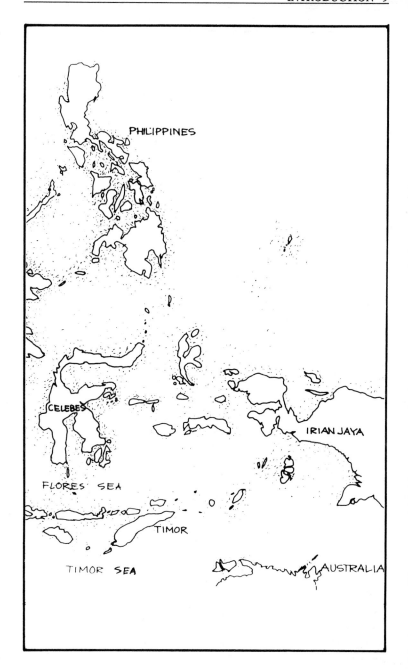

GEOGRAPHY

Nestled in the Indonesian archipelago, Bali belongs to the chain of islands that links South-east Asia with Australia, and divides the Pacific and Indian Oceans. A twinkle among the 13,677 islands in the Republic of Indonesia, Bali remains distinct in its beauty of land and of culture.

For all its fame, the tiny island is a mere 80km (50 miles) from north to south, and 150km (90 miles) at its maximum width, with an area of 5632 sq km (2095 sq miles). Located in the equatorial belt, it is 115 degrees east longitude, 8 degrees south latitude. The north and south are virtually severed by a mountainous ridge of volcanoes, the biggest being the active Gunung Agung (3142m-10,308 ft), "navel of the world" and "throne of the gods".

The Balinese are obsessed with the volcanoes. Although eruptions are devastating to the people and villages, the rich volcanic ashes regenerate the soils, and the volcanic uplands and craters help to retain the constant rain water. The volcanic terrain makes the island ideal for rice growing, and every volcano, lake and spring is revered for its life-giving qualities.

The volcanoes are also the spiritual and directional poles of Bali. *Kaja* (north) is the sacred direction, towards Gunung Agung, while *kelod* (south) is towards the diabolic sea. (Of course, to those north of the volcano, *kaja* is south.) *Kangin* (east), where the sun rises, symbolises rebirth, while *kauh* (west) where the sun sets, is associated with death. Most buildings are constructed according to these poles, and the people even sleep with their heads towards *kaja*.

Bali, in the far east of the chain of mostly volcanic islands that make up Indonesia, is adjacent to the division between Asia and Australasia.

In the 19th century, naturalist Alfred Russel Wallace, a contemporary of Darwin, posited the Wallace Line which separated Asia from Australasia on biological grounds. Bali was the eastern-most island in the chain to exhibit flora and fauna that could be classified as Asian — monkeys and even tigers, roamed in tropical jungles. Lombok, a barren, arid isle, severed from Bali by a deep strait, was home to eucalypti, parrots and marsupials akin to those found in Australia.

Bali is one of 27 provinces that make up the Republic of Indonesia, and the capital is Denpasar, situated in the south in the regency of Badung. The island is divided into eight regencies (*Kabupaten*), each governed by a *Bupati*.

CLIMATE

Placed just below the equator, Bali has a benign tropical climate. There are two seasons, a short, hot, wet season, *musim hujan*; and a longer, cooler, dry season, *musim panas*. The mountains are wet year round, averaging 2,800mm (110 inches) of rain.

The average temperature in Bali is 26C (79F) and the humidity is a relentless 75%. Generally the mountains are about 10C (50F) cooler than the coast, and in the dry season the nights can be chilly. The wet season lasts from November to March, and is the hottest time of the year with temperatures averaging 30-33C (86- 91F) by day, 24-25C (75-77F) by night. April to October is the dry season, when south-easterly winds blow from the Australian interior, easing the temperature by 2-3C (36-37F). Bali often experiences north-east and south-west monsoons, but being close to the equator is protected from typhoons and cyclones.

It's no secret that the Balinese use the sun as a clock. The island's proximity to the equator guarantees a fairly uniform 12 hours of daylight. The shortest day is in late June, the longest is in late December, and there is only about an hour's difference.

Most tourists converge on the island around December to February during peak season. This little traveller recommends visiting in the dry season — from May to September — as the island is less crowded, the weather is temperate and prices are generally cheaper.

HISTORY

Prehistory

While the Balinese trace their origins to the divine, historians view matters differently. The forebears of the Balinese probably migrated to South-east Asia from southern China around 2500 BC. These nomads scattered to various points in the archipelago, mingling with other peoples to become the "Malay" race. Stone Age relics suggest that small bands of hunter-gatherers roamed the island.

By the Bronze Age (300BC), the island was well-populated with small villages that practised farming, and possibly even wet-rice cultivation. The people worshipped various gods who presided over the elements and *cili*, the effigy of the rice goddess Dewi Sri, may have originated from a rice cult at this time. Thrones, sarcophagi and pyramids, all hewn from stone, suggest a sophisticated Megalithic culture had developed. But of all the archaeological finds pertaining to this time, the decorative bronze gong, the "Moon of Pejeng" is the most significant. Enshrined in the Pura Panataran in Pejeng, in the regency of Gianyar, the gong is the largest single cast bronze object found in Asia and dates from around 300BC. The motifs that decorate the drum suggest the influences of the Dongson bronze culture of Indo-china.

Towards Hinduism

Indian and Chinese traders had been visiting the archipelago for a thousand years, attracted by spices, sandalwood and gold. So much so, that by the 5th century, Hindu and Buddhist kingdoms were thriving in West Java and Borneo. Bali, having nothing to offer in the way of spices, lacking a suitable harbour, and being almost inaccessible, was probably not on the traders' itinerary. So, historians surmise, the Balinese probably acquired Hindu concepts and artistic motifs from the Javanese, rather than from the Indians themselves.

Most of Bali's history before the advent of stone and copperplate inscriptions, is sheer speculation. The earliest inscriptions date back to the 9th century, and as most are written in Sanskrit (ancient Indian) and Old Javanese (*Kawi*), it is probable that Bali was exposed to Hinduism by this time.

In the 11th century, the relationship between Bali and Java intensified with the Warmadewa Dynasty. The Javanese king, Dharmawangsa, probably arranged for his sister, Princess Mahendradatta, to marry the Balinese prince, Udayana (after whom the university at Denpasar is named). The couple's son, the illustrious Prince Erlangga, ruled a province of eastern Java from 1019 to 1042, while his brother, Anak Wangsa, controlled Bali. From this time all Balinese edicts were written in Old Javanese, and the Hindu epics *Ramayana* and *Mahabharata* were also translated into the language.

Majapahit Empire

During the 13th century, the Hindu Majapahit Empire established a powerful kingdom in Java. In 1343, the Javanese Prime Minister, Gajah Mada, was ordered to subdue the Balinese King Bedulu of Pejeng near Gianyar who refused to recognise Javanese sovereignty. Accompanied by Hindu nobles, Gaja Mada conquered Bedulu, and founded a Javanese court nearby, at Samprangan, near Gianyar. Sri Dalem Kapakisan, a Javanese noble, was installed as vassal ruler over Bedulu's kingdom.

The introduction of the *Triwangsa* caste system is usually ascribed to this period. The ruling caste, *Satrya*, and priestly caste, *Brahmana*, were Javanese nobles, while the third class, the *Wesya*, were probably land-holding Javanese. The indigenous Balinese were not actually included in the system and were called *Sudra*, or more popularly, *Jaba* (outsiders). The Balinese who refused to participate in the separation of society fled to the mountains, and today they are known as the *Bali Aga* or "original Balinese".

In the late 15th century, as Islamic influences spread

through Java, the Hindu Majapahit Empire was threatened with political extinction. Rather than submit to the new Islamic Mataram kingdom, the entire Majapahit entourage fled to Bali. The son of the last emperor assembled courtiers, priests, scholars and artists, and crossed the narrow strait separating Java from Bali. Popular opinion suggests that this "exodus" firmly established Hinduism in Bali.

The emperor's son bestowed upon himself the title of Dewa Agung, "Lord of Lords", and in 1515, he established a court at Gelgel near the town of Gianyar. The Dewa Agung unified Bali and the realm was extended as far as Lombok and Sumbawa. And with political prosperity came the "Golden Age". The Majapahit Empire blossomed culturally in Java, and the renaissance continued in Bali.

Hindu Bali's relationship with Islamic Java waned. While some parts of Western Bali absorbed Islamic influences, the relative isolation, lack of harbours and trade possibilities precluded most of Bali from the "onslaught" of Islam. Today, most Javanese are Muslim, while Bali lives on as a legacy of 15th century Hindu Java.

Over time, the Majapahit nobles increased their power and wealth and as the ruling classes expanded, new realms evolved. By the 18th century there were nine distinct kingdoms: Klungkung, Karangasem, Bangli, Gianyar, Buleleng, Mengwi, Badung, Tabanan and Jembrana. The kingdoms were more or less independent, while acknowledging Klungkung's Dewa Agung as the ultimate ruler.

Dutch Aspirations

In 1602, the Dutch established the Dutch East India Trading Company in western Java. Keen to exploit the spices found in parts of the archipelago, they organised trading posts in Sumatra, Borneo and the Moluccas, and Jakarta was laid to waste and rebuilt as Batavia.

Bali had little to offer the Dutch — only impenetrable jungles and perilous reefs. Fragmented records indicate that

Dutch relations with Bali involved the supply of slaves which was orchestrated by the Balinese rajas. The Dutch East India Trading Company also had the odd skirmish with opium runners, but it was the Chinese who took interest in the supply of opium and, in fact, the currency of southern China, the *kepeng*, was the only money used in Bali at this time.

In the 19th century, Bali entered the limelight. Many trade ships passed by eastern Bali and some foundered on the reefs. This was Balinese territory, and the locals had taken to plundering the wrecks which they regarded as gifts from the gods. As the Dutch controlled the archipelago, and many of the trade ships sailed under their flag, the Dutch felt they had to do something to stop the plundering. In 1846, after another case of looting (to make matters worse, a Dutch ship), the Dutch regent, accompanied by a small garrison, visited Buleleng to negotiate with the Raja. The Dutch were received with hostility, and returning to Java they prepared for an invasion.

Dutch expeditions (1846-1850)

The first Dutch military "expedition" set out to control Buleleng with 23 warships, mortars, and 3000 men armed with rifles. The Balinese, armed only with spears and *kris* (ceremonial swords), attempted to resist. The palace at Singaraja was razed and 400 Balinese lost their lives. Mads Lange, a Danish trader stationed in Kuta, intervened on behalf of the Balinese and sued for peace. The Balinese rajas signed a treaty of submission, and a Dutch garrison was posted in Buleleng with the main Dutch force leaving the island.

In 1848, another Dutch expedition was launched, as the Balinese rajas refused to abide by the terms of the treaty. Gusti Ketut Djilantik, brother to the Rajas of Buleleng and Karangasem, lured the Dutch to a fortress at Jagaraga, and in a brilliant strategic manoeuvre, surrounded them. Most of the Dutch force escaped, and returned home to prepare for war.

The third Dutch military expedition arrived in Buleleng in 1849 with the largest assembled force ever used in the archipelago: 5000 infantrymen, 3000 mercenaries, and a fleet of 60 ships with 300 sailors. Much to the surprise of the Dutch, the Balinese requested peace negotiations. A treaty was drafted ensuring Dutch control of the realm, stipulating Balinese withdrawal to Jagaraga, where they would relinquish control to the Dutch.

The Balinese returned to Jagaraga and promptly mobilised, but the Dutch were more than prepared, and swiftly trounced them. Djilantik and the Rajas of Buleleng and Karangasem fled to the mountains, and the Dutch returned home, leaving a strong force to control the new territory. Not content with half of Bali, the Dutch returned yet again, landing at Kusumba with the intention of marching to Karangasem. Djilantik and his brother, the Raja of Buleleng, organised a huge force, but this time the Balinese were brutally defeated. The Raja of Karangasem, foreseeing defeat, elected *puputan*, honourable suicide in battle. The Balinese believed that by dying in battle, the soul could reach a state of *nirvana*. And so the Court of Karangasem was no more.

In 1882, The Netherlands East-Indies government officially controlled Buleleng in the north, and Jembrana in the west. Slavery was abolished, as was the custom of *suttee*, where widows joined their husbands on the funeral pyre. The Dutch also intervened in the opium trade — ostensibly to curb the traffic — but only succeeded in creating their own monopoly!

The south was a different story. The rajas were engaged in power plays, and by the 1880s, Badung and Tabanan had destroyed the regency of Mengwi, splitting the domain between themselves. The rajas, already disgruntled with the Dutch, grew uneasy after an incident in Lombok, where the Dutch intervened in the rajas' control of the Muslim island. The Balinese waited, the Dutch waited ... finally it happened. Another shipwreck, more looting; this time a Chinese schooner off the coast of Sanur. Via the Dutch, the owner of the craft demanded exorbitant reparations, but the Raja of Badung refused. The Dutch blockaded the coasts of Badung and Tabanan and presented the Raja of Badung with an ultimatum. Once again, the raja refused and the Dutch invaded.

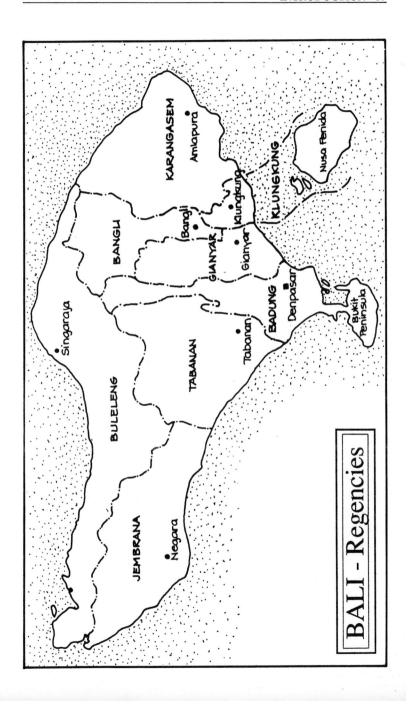

Puputan

It was September 14, 1906. The Dutch met little resistance as they marched to Denpasar. Upon their arrival they were ominously greeted by a seemingly deserted village, except for the solemn beat of drums. The palace gates were flung open and a procession of courtiers, priests, women and children, resplendent in white cremation garments was led by the Raja. Not far from the battalion, the Raja halted the procession, gave a signal, and a priest plunged a dagger into the Raja's breast. Another *puputan*. Everywhere there was death, mayhem, looting and sacking.

The Dutch advanced to Permacutan, then to Tabanan. Again and again, the Dutch were met by sacrifice. Finally, in 1908, a battalion was sent to Klungkung, the palace of the Dewa Agung and nominal capital of Bali, demanding that he surrender all power. The palace gates were opened and the Dewa Agung led his sacrificial retinue before the Dutch troops. The last bastion of Balinese royalty died as they had lived, with pomp and ceremony. In less than 16 months the Dutch had annihilated an empire that had flourished for six centuries.

Back in Holland, officials were horrified with reports of the *puputans*. In the ensuing years, the Dutch instigated a number of "benevolent" reforms. They built schools, roads and clinics, and installed a western-style system of justice. They dusted off historic monuments and generally endeavoured to tidy up — perhaps in the morning-after-the-night-before fashion!

European scholars were invited to study the Balinese culture, and reports of an idyllic island in the tropics attracted many visitors. Tourists were tolerated, but not encouraged, as the Dutch wanted to protect the Balinese from outsiders. But, by the 1930s, influential people like the German painter Walter Spies, the Dutch painter Rudolf Bonnet and the Mexican painter Miguel Covarrubias had made Bali their home. The Dutch were criticised for their exploitation of the Balinese, but peace prevailed.

Independence

During the Second World War, the Japanese occupied the island, but intervened little in local politics. After the war, the Dutch were ready to resume control, but the Indonesians had a different idea: independence. On August 17, 1945, Sukarno, the national leader, declared independence. Of course, the Dutch were not about to relinquish the colony and a war of independence, fought mostly in Java, lasted four years. One particular battle fought at Marga, on Bali, saw a modern-day *puputan*, and the leader, Ngurah Rai, a modern-day hero.

On December 29, 1949, The Hague granted independence and Bali became part of The Republic of the United States of Indonesia. Sukarno was president, answerable only to Queen Juliana of The Netherlands, but nevertheless Indonesia was free. The Dutch withdrew in 1956, and in 1963 were ejected from Irian Jaya, thereby losing their last hold on Indonesia.

But independence had its price, and the new republic was fraught with problems. The few schools, roads and hospitals, built by the Dutch were destroyed in the war. The Sukarno administration was awry financially — inflation was 100% and there were whispers of corruption. Martial law was imposed in 1957 following unsuccessful coups, and in 1963, backed by the Nationalist Party, the Communist party (PKI), and the military, Sukarno had a less than successful "confrontation" with Malaya.

Bali was affected by poor economic conditions and the unstable political structure. Land reforms dictated that no one could own more than 7.5 ha and while many of the Balinese relinquished their land, it was not equitably redistributed. The infrastructure of village life began to crumble, and being remote and Hindu, Bali was neglected by Jakarta.

The Balinese were increasingly discontented. In 1962, a plague of rats devastated crops and the people knew the gods were displeased. In February 1963, the Balinese were preparing themselves for the celebration of *Eka Dasa Rudra*, a ritual of purification held every hundred years at the Mother

Temple at Besakih. By March 8, smoke was issuing forth from the volcano — an ominous omen. Some wanted to postpone the ceremony, but Sukarno was expected, as were delegates from overseas. The initial celebrations ensued, Sukarno didn't show, the delegates left, and Gunung Agung blew! Thousands perished, 10,000 were homeless, but news of the disaster was suppressed, and aid was late and erratic.

Bali was suffering physically, Jakarta politically. On September 30, 1965, a small group kidnapped and killed six generals. Some Communist Party (PKI) members seized the radio station in Jakarta, and declared a coup d'etat. Seeing an opportunity, the Indonesian army, led by Suharto, seized control. The coup lasted 24 hours, the bloodshed continued for six months. The PKI was outlawed. A massive purge throughout Indonesia ensued, with Bali in the midst of it. Entire villages were destroyed and accounts put the deaths at 40,000. President Sukarno continued as leader until the election of Suharto in 1968. Since then, the government's party, *Golkar*, has been elected five times, without any real challengers. Of the three legal political parties, only *Golkar* has the power to organise voting and registration.

President Suharto is accountable only to the People's Consultative Assembly, of which he can choose the members — the very body that elects him.

Nonetheless, Suharto has made broad commitments to economic reforms and in the international arena, Indonesia is seen as working towards a more liberal political and economic system. Indonesia's rapid economic growth over the past two decades coupled with the upsurge in foreign investment has spurred Australia to improve its relationship with its once estranged neighbour. The highly successful Today Indonesia 94 promotion illustrated the improved ties between Australia and Indonesia, and bodes well for their future relationship.

Bali, of course, is only an extra on the set of this multi-million dollar blockbuster. In 1979, at the Besakih complex, a successful *Eka Dasa Rudra* was staged with no ominous rumblings from Agung. Since then, tourism has soared and Bali is now relatively prosperous.

THE PEOPLE

In the 1990 census, Bali was recorded as having a population of 2.7 million. The population is almost entirely Indonesian, 95 per cent of whom are Balinese Hindu. Indonesians are mainly derived from the Malay-type peoples that migrated from southern China to South-east Asia, New Guinea and Australia around 3000BC.

The Caste System

In the 14th century, when Gaja Mada and the Javanese nobles of the Majapahit empire arrived on Bali, they brought with them a version of the Hindu caste system.

The *Brahmana* were the priestly caste, the *Satrya*, the warrior-kings, and *the Wesya*, the merchants; and together they were the *Triwangsa*.

The remaining 90% of the population, the Balinese, were *Sudra*, not recognised as a caste by the ruling classes, and more commonly referred to as *Jaba* or "outsiders". The few Balinese who refused to belong to Hindu society fled inland, and today they are known as the *Bali Aga*, referring to themselves as the *original Balinese*.

The *Sudra* lived a feudal existence, and were dependent on a Hindu overlord who was supposedly endowed with divine rights. The caste system was strictly adhered to, and women were forbidden on pain of death to marry below their caste; men were merely punished.

Today, the Balinese Hindu caste system is not as rigid as its Indian precedent, and social mobility is possible. Although the *Brahmana* women are still forbidden to marry below their caste, inter-caste marriages are increasing in number, and the *Sudra* are able to enter the professional arena.

The caste system is deeply embedded in the Balinese psyche, and while legally, discrimination by caste is forbidden, the system is inextricably bound to the Balinese identity. In fact, in new encounters a name betrays caste.

Naming

Traditionally, there are no family names; rather people's names reflect their caste as well as their order of birth.

The *Brahmana* are called Ida Bagus and Ida Ayu for males and females, respectively; *Satrya* are named Cokorde, Anak Agung, and Prebagus for men; and Anak Agung Isti and Dewa Ayu for women. *Wesya* are named I Gusti and Pregusti for men; and I Gusti Ayu for women. The *Sudra* are simply I for men and Ni for women.

To signify order of birth, *Brahmana* and *Satrya* may be called Putu, Raka, or Kompiang, for the firstborn; Rai for the second; Oka for the third and Alit for the fourth. *Sudra* children are named Wayan, Made, Nyoman and Ketut, repeating the order for the fifth child. Children also have their own special name.

To complicate matters, names may change. When parents have a new child, names may change to reflect the new addition, so that they become "mother of", or "grandfather of".

The Family

Distinction according to sex is more stringent than according to class.

In the village limits, women and men have separate tasks. Only men make handicrafts, tend cattle, cook meat and cultivate the fields, whereas women do the housework, look after the pigs and chickens, cook vegetables and rice, and prepare offerings to the gods. The exception being that everyone helps with the harvesting of rice. Nonetheless, women are encouraged to participate in income-earning activities and may dispose of their independent salaries as they desire.

The men are employed to build Balinese-style constructions, but women and girls will be encountered, with

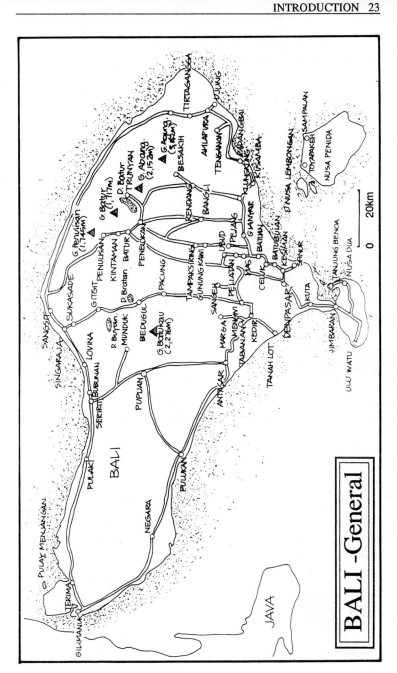

BALI -General

huge stone and cement slabs balanced on their heads, walking to western-style building sites. While women carry their wares on their heads, men carry their loads on poles balanced on their shoulders - maybe that's why the Balinese are so elegantly postured.

Today, women have the same opportunities for education as their male counterparts and are entering the professions. In fact, there's a government department in Denpasar established to lift the status of women. Although women are expected to live with their husband's family, if she should divorce (which is rare) she must leave the children and return to her own family. But during menstruation women are separated from other family members, often sleeping in a different compound. And you may notice that menstruating women are forbidden to enter temples - this is because it is sacrilege for blood to be spilt on hallowed ground.

The Village

Traditionally, the social organisation of the island is based on the village (*desa adat*), a complex network of religious, social and economic associations. Within each village are a number of *banjar* or neighbourhoods, and within each *banjar* are family compounds which extend the clan beyond parents and children.

Each member of the family belongs to a number of groups. Before marriage, an individual belongs to either a boys' or girls' club, and has specific duties as a member. Upon marrying, the person then joins the *banjar*, the irrigation association, music clubs and various other groups, and accepts the obligations that accompany membership. In this way, every individual participates fully within the social, religious and economic framework of the village. Indeed, to the Balinese, the group rather than the individual is important. Solitude is not something that the Balinese desire, and those left alone fear visits from mischievous spirits.

Most villages are organised according to spatial orientation, and the most important points of reference are *kaja* (towards Gunung Agung) and *kelod* (seawards). Each village has three temples arranged according to these directions. The *pura desa*, literally the "temple of the village", stands in the centre of the village, while at the northern end of the village is the *pura puseh*, a "temple of origin" dedicated to the spirits of the land. Both of these temples are oriented to *kaja* and the sacred Gunung Agung. On the other hand, the *pura dalem* or "temple of the dead", as well as the village burial ground, face *kelod*.

On a smaller scale, the family compound is also planned in relation to the mountains and sea.

The governing body of each neighbourhood is the *banjar*, a democratic association of married men, who make all the decisions pertaining to the village. The *banjar bale* is the meeting place for the *banjar* as well as all villagers: feasts are prepared, games are held, and dances practised. Sometimes the villagers even sleep there.

LANGUAGE

The average Balinese who deals with tourists is usually conversant with one of the Balinese dialects as well as the "language of courtesies", Bahasa Indonesia (the official language of Indonesia) and English.

The "language of courtesies" is a complex Balinese language which employs three different levels to indicate the caste or status of the listener: low or *kasar*; middle or *mider*; and high or *alus*. *Kasar*, known as common Balinese, is a Malay-Polynesian dialect. The strange thing is, that when a person of high caste addresses a person of low caste, the high caste will speak in *kasar* and the low caste person will use *alus*.

Although English is widely spoken and most children are

taught English at school from the age of 12, Bahasa Indonesia is fast becoming the *lingua franca*.

Bahasa Indonesia

Bahasa Indonesia, which evolved from a Malay dialect spoken in Sumatra, has much in common with other Malay dialects. Since it is a relatively simple and widely-used language, and is not associated with one of the dominant ethnic groups in Indonesia, it has been accepted without serious question. Indeed, it has served as a strong force of national unification. Bahasa Indonesia is taught in most schools, is widely used by the media, and in Bali it is becoming preferable to Balinese.

In 1972, a uniform revised spelling was agreed upon between Indonesia and Malaysia so that communications would improve and literature could be freely exchanged between the nations.

If you're staying on the island, try learning a few words, it's really quite easy. There are basically seven vowel signs each of which has only one pronunciation.
(English has five vowel symbols, but they generate over 20 different sounds.)

a as in cut
e as in set
i as in me
o as in not
u as in you
ai as in bike
au as in now

The consonants are similar to English consonants, but here are a few minor exceptions.
c is "ch" as in chip, but
k is "c" as in car
g as in girl
ng as in ring
h as in help, but with more breath, and it is silent at the end of

a word

r is always rolled as "rrr"

The rules for grammar are also quite simple. Sentences are usually ordered: subject, verb, object. There are no articles, like "a" or "the". There are no tenses for verbs (well, none that tourists need learn), as time is indicated by context rather than an inflected form; for instance, words like yesterday (kemarin) and tomorrow (besok) are placed at the beginning of a sentence to indicate time. Questions are usually indicated by question words, but sometimes by raising the pitch of the voice at the end of the sentence. It's also possible to make a question by adding "Kah" to the end of the word which asks the question. Do not try and use this form until you feel comfortable with the language - you can get by without it. Generally, the last syllable of a word is emphasised.

If you want to impress the locals, here are a few words.

Pronouns

I/my - *saya*
you - *kamu*
he/she - *dia*
we - *kami*
they - *mereka*

Titles

Miss - *nona*
Mr - *bapak*
Mrs - *ibu*
Sir - *tuan*
Madam - *nyonya*
child - *anak*

Greetings and Civilities

good morning - *selamat Pagi*
good afternoon (11am-3pm) - *selamat siang*

good afternoon (after 3pm) - *selamat sore*
goodnight - *selamat malam*
sleep well - *selamat tidur*
goodbye (when leaving) - *selamat tinggal*
goodbye (when staying) - *selamat jalan*
please - *silahkan*
thank you - *terima kasih*
you're welcome - *sama sama*
 sorry - *ma'af* ; (and another is)   excuse me - *permisi*

Questions

what - *apa*
who - *siapa*
when - *kapan*
where is - *dimana ada*
where to - *kemana*
from where - *darimana*
how - *bagaimana*
why - *mengapa*
may I - *boleh*
How are you - *Apa kabar?*

Useful Words

well - *baik baik*
good - *bagus*
bad - *jahat*
sick - *sakit*
wrong - *salah*
no - *tidak* (in front of verbs -
but interchangeable with *bukan*)
no - *bukan* (in front of nouns)
not yet - *belum*
walk and street/walking - jalan/jalan jalan
village - *desa*

like - *sukar*
there is - *ada*
this - *ini*
want (will or shall) - *mau*

Useful Phrases

I want it - *saya mau*
I do not want it - *saya tidak mau*
What is your name - *siapa nama*
My name is... - *nama saya...*

Quantity

all - *semua*
some - *lain*
little - *sedikit*
many - *banyak*

Time

today (this day) - *hari ini*
tonight (this night) - *malam ini*
yesterday - *kemarin*
tomorrow - *besok*
week - *minggu*
month - *bulan*
year - *tahun*

Shopping

What's this - *Apa ini*
How much - *berapa*
money - *rupiah*
cheap - *murah*
expensive - *mahal*

Food

food - *makam*
drink - *minum*
chicken - *ayam*

noodles - *mei*
salt - *garam*
pepper - *merica* sweet - *manis*

fish - *ikan*

pork - *babi*

fruit - *buah*

rice - *nasi*

sour - *asam*

sugar - *gula*

milk - *susu*

tea/coffee - *teh/kopi*

Numbers

1 - *satu*

2 - *dua*

3 - *tiga*

4 - *empat*

5 - *lima*

6 - *enam*

7 - *tujuh*

8 - *delapan*

9 - *sembilan*

10 - *supuluh*

11 - *sebelas*

12 - *duabelas20 - duapuluh*

30 - *tigapuluh*

100 - *seratus*

101 - *seratus satu*

1000 - *seribu*

2000 - *duaribu*

10,000 - *sepuluh ribu*

20,000 - *duapuluh ribu*

Literature

Most literature is derived from Sanskrit which was translated into Old Javanese or *Kawi* around the 10th century. At that time, the Javanese prince, Erlangga (who ruled Bali through his brother), declared that all Balinese edicts should be translated into *Kawi*. Erlangga also oversaw the translations of the two great Hindu epic poems, the *Ramayana* and the *Mahabharata* from Sanskrit. Today only *dalang* (shadow puppeteers), priests and the older Balinese understand *Kawi*, but the language is still celebrated in the puppet shows of the *Wayang Kulit*, in the modern *Ramayana* ballet, *Wayang Wong*, and in excerpts staged in dances and dramas.

The *Ramayana* is an old-fashioned story of the struggle between good and evil. Rama, the hero, embodies virtue and strength, while his antagonist, Rawana, epitomises evil. The *Mahabharata* recalls the exploits and deeds in the battle of the Bharatas (from ancient northern India).

BALINESE HINDUISM

Signs of Hindu devotion are everywhere. Small gifts of flowers and rice, scrupulously prepared, are laid on the dashboard of a bemo, or on the counter of a boutique. Women and girls, resplendent in *sarong* and *kebaya* place offerings in temples, hotels and crossroads. They stop awhile to pray, or perhaps light incense to attract the attention of the gods. Small clues to the spiritual life of the Balinese.

Most Balinese practise a variation of the Hindu religion called *Agama Hindu Dharma* (the Religion of the Hindu Doctrine) but sometimes known as *Agama Tirtha* (the Religion of Holy Water). Balinese Hinduism is a unique mixture of Buddhism and Hinduism, combined with a pinch of animism from centuries past. The basic tenet of Hindu Dharma is that the soul (*atman*) is reincarnated after death. In what form, depends on personal actions or *karma*, and eventually, a soul may achieve unity with the divine (*moksa*).

The Balinese practise their faith with an earthy exuberance, endeavouring to achieve a balance between philosophy, morals and rituals. And balance is everything.

The Balinese are aware of the ever-present forces of good and evil. One cannot exist without the other, and indeed, nothing but a balance between the two will prevent chaos. The people live between the gods and the demons — endeavouring to please one, and appease the other.

Cosmic stability depends on the co-existence of opposites. In the same way, everything is born, dies and is reborn. The soul lives in the heavens or on the earth. Volcanoes erupt and kill, and later the volcanic ash provides fertile loams for cultivation. And those mangy dogs (*cecing*) that howl all night and devour offerings, are merely evil spirits put on earth to balance all things beautiful. The notion of opposites is epitomised in the *kaja-kelod* axis.

Contrary to popular opinion, the educated Hindus subscribe to a monotheistic religion. Ida Sanghyang Widi is the supreme god capable of many manifestations, the most notable being the holy trinity or *tri murti*: Brahma, the creator; Wisnu, the preserver; and Siwa, the destroyer. Belief in one God is the first of the five principles of the Republic of Indonesia, known as the *pancasila*. Even so, the average Balinese, not troubled with resolving a plethora of Hindu gods with the (Islamic) notion of one god, acknowledges a multitude of different deities who watch over the family, village and land.

Temples

Bali has been called the "land of a thousand temples" — what an understatement! Bali might be a small island, but there are many, many more than a thousand temples. Every village has at least three temples, a family compound has one, each rice growing co-operative (*subak*) has a temple, even corporations have them. Some are simple affairs, others are elaborate sprawling complexes of major and minor temples, incorporating pagodas and shrines.

The three important village temples are: the *pura puseh* ("temple of origin"); the *pura desa* ("village temple") in the centre; and the *pura dalem* ("temple of the dead"). The temple of origin is associated with Brahma the creator, and faces Gunung Agung, towards *kaja*, as does the village temple which is associated with Wisnu, the preserver. The temple of the dead is the domain of Siwa, the destroyer, and faces the sea, *kelod*.

Although no two temples are the same, many do share similarities in design. Most temples have three courtyards, each with a split gate entrance, known as a *candi bentar*. The first courtyard is open and spacious with a number of small pavilions (*bale*) where people assemble for prayer and ceremonial preparations. The second courtyard is much the same, while the inner sanctum is the abode of the gods. Leading to the inner courtyard is a set of doors. Open the doors and a wall prevents you from moving forward — you can step either to the left or to the right. The wall is an *aling aling* and it prevents spirits from entering the courtyard because it's thought that spirits have great problems negotiating corners! Within this courtyard are a number of *meru* shrines which line the northern and eastern walls. The multi-tiered *meru* have odd-numbered roofs, depending on the god to which they are dedicated. Located in the north-east corner is the lotus throne. This is a *padmasana*, the seat of Ida Sanghyang Widi, the supreme god. If there are three thrones, they are dedicated to the supreme god's manifestations as Brahma, Wisnu and Siwa.

Each temple has a *pemangku* who maintains the compound and anyone, regardless of sex or caste, can become one. The high priest, or *pedanda*, presides over ceremonies, and must be of the *brahmana* caste.

Rites of Passage

The Balinese believe that the individual soul is reincarnated several times until it achieves unity with the divine (*moska*). Of course, it takes some individuals a little longer than others to attain *moska* — depending on their deeds or misdeeds (*karma*). When the soul is in the heavens, between incarnations, the gods protect it; but when on earth, its welfare is the business of the Balinese. From birth to death, Bali's Hindus conduct important rites to guide the soul through its various stages.

The rites of passage begin while the child is still in the womb. A pregnant woman is "ritually unclean" (*sebel*) and is not permitted to enter a temple. When the child is delivered, the afterbirth is buried to attract spiritual guides from each of the four cardinal directions to accompany the child throughout its life. There are further rites for the child at 12 days and at 42 days. After 105 days, the child is placed on the ground for the first time and Mother Earth, *Ibu Pertiwi*, is asked to protect it. Before the ceremony the child is not regarded as a human being -in fact, the child's soul is more divine than human, as it has just come from the realm of the gods. And at 210 days (one Balinese year) the child is named. One thing you'll never see is a Balinese baby crawling. They are not allowed to crawl, as do animals, so babies are carried everywhere until they can walk.

The passage into puberty is celebrated for both males and females with the tooth-filing ceremony. The ritual must be completed before marriage, and these days it is often incorporated into the marriage ritual. The canine teeth are considered to be animalistic, so they are filed, and this symbolises the levelling of the volatile and beastly aspects of an individual's personality.

Once the daughter has had her teeth filed, her father is no longer obligated to her. However, the father of a son must finance and conduct his son's wedding ceremony, welcoming the bride as his daughter; and the bride must accept her new family and their family gods. A few Balinese marriages are pre-arranged (with the consent of the boy and girl), and fewer still are mixed-caste marriages. The preferred method of entering into wedlock is characteristically Balinese: it is at once dramatic and pragmatic.

Many young men prefer to "kidnap" their brides. The boy "seizes" the girl and after feigned resistance on her part, he carries her off to a pre-arranged retreat. Of course, her family are suitably outraged by the incident, and her father may organise a mock search party to locate her whereabouts - to no avail. The couple make offerings to the gods and consummate the marriage before the offerings wither. Days later, the bride's father will grudgingly relinquish his daughter, but not without payment. The official nuptials, celebrated by the groom's village priest, are merely a formality as the couple have already married in the eyes of the gods.

Cremation

Cremation of the dead is the most important ritual for the Balinese because it liberates the soul from the confines of the body. The body is merely a temporary and unclean vehicle for the soul whose real home is with the gods. The entire ritual is colourful, noisy and exuberant. No expense is spared, and preparations are undertaken with fervour and care. If the cremation is not organised and conducted as the Hindu edicts dictate, the deceased's soul may wander the earth perpetrating mischief, or return to haunt the family who did not undertake the cremation correctly.

Because of the preparation and cost involved, cremation ceremonies are the privilege of a few, and sometimes group rituals are held. In either case the body is interred until the ceremony, or if the ceremony occurs quickly the body is held in the family compound. During this time in limbo, the soul is said to be agitated, eager to resume life with the gods.

The village priest consults the Balinese calender and chooses an auspicious date. The family then constructs a large tower of bamboo and paper, and decorates it according to the caste and wealth of the deceased. Sometimes the body is enshrined in a life-size bull, built of bamboo and plaster.

On the appointed morning, relatives and friends of the deceased visit the family home to pay their respects. At noon, a procession of family and friends, not to mention well-wishers, a *gamelan* orchestra and anybody who cares to join in, leads the tower to the graveyard. Sometimes there are as many as a hundred bearers, bedecked in white ceremonial robes. The family guide the tower with long strips of white fabric. The vital consideration in all this, is that the soul not return home. And with this in mind, the *gamelan* plays thunderously, the people cheer, and the tower is rotated several times - all to confuse the soul and prevent it from escaping before its delivery to the gods.

At the graveyard, the body is placed inside the bull, or sometimes laid on a mound and wrapped in palm leaves. A priest officiates, chanting the last rites, and then the pyre is lit. Afterwards the ashes are collected, and another procession leads to the sea where the remains are thrown to the wind, representing a cleansing of the soul and disposal of the body. The soul sojourns in heaven before returning to earth in a different body. As mentioned, the status of the reborn soul depends on *karma*, or the soul's conduct in the previous life.

A ceremony to end all ceremonies, a cremation is not a time for tears — the soul is freed from the bondage of the material life and draws closer to unity with the divine — it is a time for celebration. The splendour of the ceremony, the colours, music, incense, fire — all augment the excitement for the passage of the soul from this life to the next.

The Balinese have certainly caught up with technology, though. Some ceremonies use elaborate loud-speaker systems to transmit the rites, and capture the moment on videotape for posterity.

THE BALINESE CALENDAR

Keeping an appointment in Bali can be confusing. The Balinese calender year is arranged according to two parallel systems; the 12 month lunar calendar and the *wuku* or *pawukon* calendar. Festivals are held on auspicious days for both calendars as well as days where the calendars co-incide. Every day is associated with benevolent or malevolent forces, which must be considered before undertaking any activity. To complicate matters, the Gregorian Calendar, which is based on the solar year and is attuned to the changing seasons, is also used.

The lunar calendar is based on the phases of the moon, similar to the system used in India. Each month has 29 or 30 days to adjust to the moons cycle of 29.5 days; and each month begins the day following the new moon, which means the full moon occurs mid-cycle. Twelve *sasih* months comprise a year, and an extra thirteenth month is added every three or four years to compensate for the longer solar year in the Gregorian Calendar.

The *wuku* calender is originally Balinese, and probably derives from the cultivation period of rice. The year lasts 210 days, and every day has its own god, constellation of the stars, and omen. The *wuku* year is subdivided into shorter cycles that run concurrently. The most important of these are the three, five and seven-day weeks whose conjunctions determine most holy days.

Here are the dates for Galungan and Kuningan respectively:

1994 —	2 November;	12 November
1995 —	31 May;	10 June
1996 —	24 July;	3 August
1997 —	19 February;	1 March

Festivals and Holy Days

Each temple has an anniversary, and as there are thousands of temples, there is at least one festival every day. The Badung Government Tourist Office in Denpasar publishes a monthly list of imminent temple festivals, available at most tourist centres.

Odalan

This is a temple's anniversary celebration and occurs once each *wuku* year. Preparations for the much-awaited event begin weeks before, and everyone, but everyone, participates. The temple is given a spring-clean and decorated, and large ornate offerings are created. On the first day, the women carry offerings to the temple, resplendent in elegant ceremonial costume, balancing huge baskets of fruit on their heads. In the temple, the priests bless the offerings with holy water, proffering them to the gods and the spirits who devour their essence. Three days later, the pragmatic Balinese are entitled to the leftovers. During the three-day celebrations, the temple compound is enlivened with food stalls, markets, cockfights and music. Toys, balloons and other colourful paraphernalia are not an uncommon sight. At night, dances, shadow-puppet plays and dramas are performed.

Galungan

The most auspicious of festivals, it celebrates the creation of the world by the supreme God and celebrates the triumph of good over evil. It is a day of feasting, and re-union with one's family. Should you see *penjor*, bamboo poles decorated with flowers, swaying over roads, you can be sure *Galungan* is near.

Kuningan

This is held ten days after *Galungan* and brings the festival to a close. *Kuningan* honours the souls of favoured ancestors and deities — a kind of "All Souls Day".

Nyepi

This is the Balinese new year in the lunar calendar. A holy day, it falls on the spring equinox and is observed as a day of silence. On the eve of *Nyepi*, clamorous rites of purification and exorcism frighten the old-year spirits out of their wits. Then, on the day of *Nyepi*, there's silence. No-one ventures outside, no fires can be lit, no work done, and above all no noise. The deathly stillness will convince all the spirits that the island has been deserted and they'll flee. It's expected that some spirits won't be fooled and will return next year.

THE PERFORMING ARTS

Some claim that all Balinese are artists - which is probably a slight exaggeration. Nevertheless, the arts are an integral part of Balinese life and are inextricably linked to Hinduism. There are few professionals - most artists perform as an offering to the gods and for the sheer enjoyment. Poems, plays and dances are a vehicle for religious and moral instruction, as well as being just plain good fun.

Far from being traditions resurrected for the titillation of tourists, the Balinese continually experiment with different genres, creating new musical and dance forms. Indeed, the Indonesian Academy of Music and Dance, in Denpasar, was established to ensure the continued vitality and creativity of the performing arts.

Dance and Drama

The traditions of Balinese dance and drama are derived from

Hindu Java and ultimately, from India. Balinese dancing is a sophisticated and highly stylised form of entertainment. Every movement is symbolic, and is formed in harmony with every other movement, the emphasis being on the eyes, head and arms, rather than the legs. And the entire performance is bereft of emotion. The best performers are those who are inspired by the divine -they will be transported and become their character.

Some of the dances involve pure movement, others meld movement with drama, retelling myths and religious stories.

Some dances are secular, some sacred. *Wali* dances are those performed in the inner sanctum of the temple and are the most revered. The *rejang, baris* and *sanghyang* trance dances are religious, while the *legong, kecak* and *joged* dances are soley for entertainment. There are hundreds of dances in the Balinese repertoire, some are classics, others are just the flavour of the month.

The Balinese learn to dance at a very young age, some girls begin at the age of four, and unlike Westerners, they will continue to dance until they can no longer make the moves.

Here's a list of a few of the dances that visitors are likely to see.

Barong (Kris dance)

A morality play recounting the mythical struggle between the witch, Rangda, and the holy Barong. The story is based on the *Calon Arang* myth which tells of the 12th century Javanese king, Erlangga, who conquered his mother, Mahendratta, a bitter woman given to terrorising villages with her black magic. The final scene of the *barong* dance features the famous *kris* trance dance, where the Barong's warriors defeat the evil Rangda and prove the goodness of the Barong by committing suicide with their *kris* swords.

Baris

A demanding solo or group warrior dance. A strapping young warrior prepares himself for war, strutting and posturing, while assuming various stylised gestures and expressions. The warrior must exhibit the gamut of emotions equated with a soldier - dignity, ferocity, strength, contempt, and mercy.

Traditional Baris dance at Nusa Dua

Joged Bung Bung

A flirting dance accompanied by a bamboo orchestra. Originally from the regency of Buleleng, the *joged* features a beautiful young girl who encourages men from the audience to dance with her. Westerners are particular favourites, as even the most lithe and supple of men look unco-ordinated when compared to a Balinese dancer. The audience invariably roars with laughter at the antics of both.

Kebyar Deduk

Kebyar means "lightning" and the dance is one of the most strenuous of all the dance forms. The *kebyar deduk* was created by the Balinese dancer Mario, and is performed while in a seated position.

Kecak

The monkey dance. A human orchestra of one-hundred men dressed in chequered sarongs, sway rhythmically, chanting "chucka, chucka, chucka". They provide a musical backdrop to episodes performed from the *Ramayana*; usually the story of the white monkey general, Hanuman, is told, hence the "monkey dance". The dance was created by Walter Spies in the 1930s and was inspired by existing traditions.

Legong Keraton

A classical and highly abstract dance performed with exquisite grace by beautiful young girls. There are various stories which accompany the traditional *legong* dances. The dance most often performed recalls the myth of Princess Rangkesari, a beautiful maiden abducted by the king, Lasem. The king attempts to win her favours, but she refuses. When the princess's brother comes to free her, she appeals to Lasem to release her, and warns him of her brother's ferocity. Lasem keeps her captive, and when he ventures out to battle with the brother, he meets a raven, an omen of his impending death. The story finishes unconcluded.

Three girls dance this version, one introduces the story, and the other two, dressed identically, play the parts of the princess and king. The two dancers are tightly wrapped in gold brocade, flattening their bodies - the dance is extremely erotic, but visual sexuality is suppressed. Elaborate frangipani-laden crowns sit upon their heads and their impassionate faces are heavily powdered.

At one moment their movements are perfectly synchronised, the next they separate assuming different roles only to return in perfect accord. The dance is abstract and symbolic, and at times it is difficult to follow the plot.

The *legong* is probably the most difficult and famous of all the dances. The dance troupe at Peliatan, near Ubud, is said to be the best on the island.

Pendent

Originally a temple procession, danced by male and female *pegmangkus*. The dancers welcomed the gods to the festival, showering shrines with flower petals. These days, the *pendet* is performed by young girls to open dance performances.

Topeng

The name means "mask" and refers to any of the various mask dances. The dancer must convey the character of the mask through gesture and movement. Indeed, the wearer does not assume the character of the mask but is said to be possessed by the mask's spirit. This is why masks are treated with such care.

Music

The Balinese are as musical, as they are dramatic. Music is everywhere — the tones of the gamelan ringing from the local banjar, a boy playing on a *tingklik* (bamboo xylophone), Balinese women singing in the streets or doves "tinkling" overhead as the bells round their necks ring. Sometimes it's difficult to distinguish the noises of nature from those contrived by artists. In fact some historians suggest that music began centuries ago with the chanting and stomping of women harvesting rice.

Most Balinese music derives from the *gamelan*. No words can describe the captivating, electric, frenetic, percussive tones of the *gamelan*. Capable of such soft, haunting music, yet favoured for its dramatic, fast, thunderous clanging. Some visitors to the island can never appreciate or become attuned to the *gamelan*, mistaking its rippling complexities for a cacophonous din. Many Western musicians are amazed at the complexities of Balinese music, and the likes of Mahler and later, Philip Glass, have been influenced by the *gamelan*.

The term *gamelan* (derived from "*pegamelan*" which means handler), refers to both the orchestra and the instruments. The *gamelan* orchestra is composed primarily of instruments akin to a xylophone, called *gangsa*. The keys are usually bronze placed over bamboo resonators, and beaten with a mallet. The orchestra also has a *riong*, a frame with bronze pots played by four men; a *trompong*, like a *riong* but played solo; a *cengceng* a frame with cymbals suspended from it; and *kendang*, drums.

The musicians will invariably be male, seated on the ground, and dressed in the uniform of their particular orchestra. The instruments are of invariable pitch, fixed at the time of manufacture.

The *gong kebyar* (*kebyar* means "lightning"), is probably the best known of the *gamelan* orchestras. The music is fast, jazzy and syncopated. Kettle drums, pots, gongs, drums and sometimes flutes are paired in rows, and tuned in pairs so that one of the pair is of a slightly higher pitch than the other — achieving a rippling, twinkling sound.

Puppetry

Wayang kulit, or shadow play, is the oldest performing art in Indonesia. Inscriptions suggest that it was prevalent by the 9th century, and although the Javanese certainly had puppet shows before this time, the Balinese look upon the *wayang kulit* as an indigenous art.

Probably the all-time favourite Balinese entertainment, the *wayang kulit* retells stories from the *Mahabharata* and *Ramayana*. Brightly painted puppets, crafted from cowhide and laced with holes, dance on thin bone handles. Illuminated by lamp, they cast the shadows of gods, clowns and courtiers. Each puppet is instantly recognisable as a character from the story, and each character has a symbolic purpose and stylised movements.

The puppet master or *dalang*, as well as choreographing the performance, narrates, sometimes touching on moral, philosophical, political and social problems. He (sometimes she) is the master, realising all the possible hundreds of characters, subtly combining moral instruction with entertainment. All this and the *dalang* still manages to sit cross-legged manipulating the puppets. And no performance would be complete without the dramatic tones of the *gamelan*.

ART

Painting

Some travellers visit Bali simply to buy paintings. They hop off the plane, catch a taxi to Ubud, acquaint themselves with the going prices, and then buy, buy, buy.

Balinese paintings are known for their vibrant colours, iconography, stylised figures and ornate backgrounds, and are almost certainly derived from the *wayang kulit* or shadow-puppet theatre. The similarities between the colourful, stylised puppets and the figures depicted in many paintings, illustrates the connection. Of course, the influx of Majapahit Hindus also had an impact on painting styles, not to mention Western artists.

Earliest paintings

The earliest paintings, known as the Kamasan style are traced to the 17th century kingdom of Klungkung, where *wayang kulit* figures were incorporated into paintings. Initially, the pictures adorned temples, later becoming decorations for the home. The figures are typically shown frontally, with a three-quarter view of the face rather than a profile as with the puppets. The artists used natural pigments on bark paper, wooden boards, or on woven, unbleached cloth. Themes are mainly derived from the Hindu epics, the *Ramayana* and the *Mahabharata*.

Twentieth Century

In the early 20th century, with no rajas to commission works, many painters laid their brushes to rest. Between the World Wars, a couple of Western artists who'd heard about a haven of artisans, moved to Ubud. The German, Walter Spies, and the Dutch artist, Rudolf Bonnet, established studios in Ubud, encouraging the locals to ignore set formulas, and themselves toying with traditional Balinese methods. The artists used Western-style materials and the themes were often free of religious symbolism, focusing on daily scenes. Colours were restrained, even monochrome, and the depictions comparatively realistic, although ignoring light and shade.

A new generation of Balinese painters was born — Made Griya, Gusti Njoman Lempad and Ida Bagus Anom — all with individual styles. In 1936, Spies, Bonnet and several indigenous painters founded an association called *Pita Maha* devoted to the development of the arts in Ubud, but it disintegrated with the outbreak of the Second World War.

In Batuan, at this time, artists were creating their own styles, some influenced by the Pita Maha. Batuan paintings featured fine lines, painstaking detail filling the entire canvas, and sombre greens and maroons. Themes included fables, legends, the supernatural and later, tourism. I Made Budi, is especially famous for his witty interpretations of tourism, as well as politics.

From the 1950s to the Present

In the 1950s, in Penestanan, a new style emerged influenced by the Dutch painter, Arie Smit, and the Australian Donald Friend. Characterised by strong primary colours and simple, bold lines, the paintings demonstrated a child-like joy of reality. The paintings sometimes referred to as the "naive" or "young artists" style, are extremely popular with tourists, and despite their relatively simple and quick creation, demand the same prices as more complex and technically superior paintings.

There are a few academic painters who have received formal training abroad or at the Indonesian art academies in Yogyakarta and Denpasar. These painters are dedicated to personal styles while still exhibiting Balinese influences.

> Visit the Neka Museum, Ubud (open daily from 9am to 5pm) as well as the Puri Lukisan museum on Ubud Raya.

Carving

The Balinese will carve and sculpt anything: wood, stone, bone, horn, deadwood, even roots. It seems that no stone is left unadorned, no piece of wood bare. From the ornate split gateways of the temples, to the door of your hotel, everything seems to be carved.

Traditionally, stone was carved for temples and buildings. There has always been a demand for stone carvers, because the soft volcanic *paras* used for building, although easy to sculpt, deteriorates quickly. Tourism, however, has altered demand, and many carvers have turned to wood.

Initially, the woodcarvers were *brahmana*, dedicated to carving for ritual or courtly commissions, and the tradition was passed from father to son. The traditional *wayang* style was prevalent, depicting religious characters and tales from the *Ramayana* and *Mahabharata* epics.

Under the influence of Walter Spies and the Pita Maha, the

style of carving developed to portray realistic, daily scenes. Today, painted carvings made from local soft woods are mass-produced and imitation fruit, garish *garudas* and tacky masks can be bought anywhere. Despite the mindless duplication, there are sculptures carved with genius.

The Art Centre at Denpasar and Ida Bagus Tilems's gallery at Mas, offer rare treasures.

Ebony is imported from Kalimantan and Sulawesi, and is very expensive. If you're not sure that it's ebony, see if it floats - ebony doesn't float.

Textiles

Cloth, to the Balinese, is not so much a necessity as a mark of religious and social standing. Even statues and shrines share in the sartorial splendour.

Balinese cloth is amazingly cheap and gorgeous. Buying from the markets is easy, but the best bet is to venture into the weaving factories and cloth shops. And while you're there, have a seamstress transform your purchase into a fine garment.

Batik

Hate to disappoint, but most *batik* is imported from Java. Some factories make hand-figured *batik*, particularly in Gianyar.

Endek

A tie-dyed woven cloth, *endek* is created from the *ikat* method of dyeing. Sections of the fabric are wrapped, and then the cloth is immersed in dye, the wrapped parts remaining undyed. The process can be repeated several times creating a muted, wavy pattern.

Kain Prada

These are fine fabrics of woven silk or cotton decorated with gold or silver threads. They are usually made into scarfs.

Geringsing

This is a rare method of weaving, only practised in Tenganan, Karangasem. Both the warp and the weft are dyed in what's called the *double-ikat* method. Colours are made from natural dyes, and are limited to black, red and yellow. One piece of geringsing may take a couple of years to work. Prices are around one million-rupiah range, but the cloth is extremely rare and painstakingly crafted.

Songket

This is the real ceremonial brocade. Gold and silver threads are added on the loom creating a range of patterns from simple lines to intricate lotus flowers and *wayang kulit* figures. *Songket* is sold in art shops thoughout the island.

ECONOMY

Surprisingly, less than 50% of the population are engaged in agricultural pursuits, as the chief industry is tourism. Salt panning, textiles and brickmaking are small industries, and rice, pigs, cattle, coffee, vanilla, cotton and seaweed, are all exported. Despite the fact that Bali is an island, the people have misgivings about the sea and have never been known for their maritime interests, however there is commercial fishing.

Tourism

In 1967, when General Suharto became President of the Republic of Indonesia, the World Bank advised the government to address its national debt problem through tourism — it was good advice. About 1.2 million tourists visit Bali annually creating about a third of the economy.

AGRICULTURE

It should come as no surprise that rice cultivation dominates the agricultural economy. Rice is usually rotated with other crops, such as peanuts, onions, chilli-peppers and corn.

Rice Cultivation

Rice is not only essential fare but a sacred gift. *Dewi Sri*, the rice goddess, is one of the favoured gods, and worship of this deity predates Balinese Hinduism. Heavy rainfall, natural springs, fertile volcanic loams and constant sunshine make Bali ideal for rice farming. Indeed, such agricultural prosperity has enabled the development of a complex civilisation since early times.

Since the 11th century, all people whose land was fed by the same water channel have belonged to a *subak*, or irrigation co-operative. Distinct from normal village organisations, a *subak* may co-ordinate irrigation of several villages, depending on drainage patterns. The most important duties of the co-operative include the construction of irrigation networks. Developed over the centuries, the irrigation techniques make Balinese rice farming the most sophisticated in Indonesia.

The *subak* also oversees the cultural side of cultivation. All aspects of farming are discussed with recourse to the gods and holy days, and offerings are made to *Dewi Sri* to repel vermin, locusts and evil spirits. When the rice is ready to harvest, the first propitious rice sheaves are used to make a "rice mother" effigy, known as *cili*, later enshrined in the cultivator's household temple to survey and protect the crop. At harvest time, everyone helps, working by day, celebrating by night. *Beras Bali*, the favoured strain of rice, is used primarily for ceremonies, and yields one harvest a year. The introduction of new breeds of rice capable of two or more harvests a year has almost replaced the traditional breed.

NOTES

GENERAL INFORMATION

ENTRY REGULATIONS

Visitors to Bali require a passport which is valid for a minimum of six months upon arrival and a return ticket, and passports should have an empty page to be stamped. Nationals of Australia, Canada, Ireland, New Zealand, Singapore, Thailand, United Kingdom and United States, amongst others, are permitted visa-free entry into Bali. Employment is forbidden on tourist visas or visa-free entry.

Visa-free entry requires that visitors do not exceed a stay of 60 days, and extensions are not permitted.

Health Regulations

Certificates of vaccination are not required, but health authorities advise protection against Typhoid, Malaria and Tetanus.

The water is not particularly safe for Westerners. Bottled water is recommended for drinking, and is widely available.

Customs Allowance

The following goods may be imported into Bali free of customs duty:

50 cigars, 200 cigarettes or 100 grams of tobacco. (Some people do not realise that they can pack unlimited quantities of cigarettes bought in their own country prior to travel, the limit pertains only to duty-free purchases.)

All personal effects, 2 litres of alcohol, reasonable amounts of perfume, gifts.

Cameras, video cameras, and a reasonable amount of film, typewriters, binoculars, radios and books are allowed in provided they are taken out at departure.

There is no restriction on the import of foreign currencies in cash or traveller's cheques.

The import of weapons, narcotics, Chinese medicines and literature with Chinese characters, as well as pornographic material, is forbidden.

EXIT REGULATIONS

| Departure Tax |

If leaving Bali by air, the departure tax is Rp14,000 (US$6.50) Domestic departure tax varies for different airports and is usually around Rp5,500 (US$2.50).

There is no restriction on the export of foreign currencies in cash or traveller's cheques, but the export of Indonesian currency is prohibited.

Flights should be confirmed three days before departure.

EMBASSIES

Unfortunately, most tourists who lose their passports will have to make the jaunt to Jakarta. Fortunately for *Australians,* there is a consulate in Denpasar. There is also a *United States* consular agency at Sanur. Theft or loss of passport must first be reported to the police. Keep a photocopy of your passport and driver's licence for identification at the consulate.

Here's a list of embassies and consulates.

Australia: Australian Consulate, Jl. Mochammad Yamin 51, Renon, Denpasar, P.O. Box 243, ph 235 092, 235 093.
Canada: Canadian Embassy, 5th flr, Wisma Metropolitan, Jl. Jen Sudirman, Kav 29, Jakarta, ph 51 0709.
New Zealand: New Zealand Embassy, Jl. Diponegoro 41 Jakarta, ph 33 0680.
Singapore: Block X14 KAV S3, Jl. H R Rasuna Said, Kuningan, Jakarta, ph 520 1491.
United Kingdom.: Jl. M H Thamrin 75, Jakarta, ph 33 0904.
United States: Jl. Medan Merdeka Selatan 5, Jakarta, ph 36 0360.

IMMIGRATION

The immigration office (*Kantor Imigrasi*) is in the Renon Complex, Niti Mandala, Denpasar. If you are unable to make a flight, try to apply for an extension a couple of days prior to the expiration of your entry stamp. *Office hours* are: Monday to Thursday 7am-1pm, Friday 7am-11am, Saturday 7am-noon.

> Always remember: when entering any government office, dress properly. Bureaucrats refuse to deal with tourists clad in beach gear.

MONEY

The unit of currency in Indonesia is the rupiah. Notes are in denominations of 100, 500, 1000, 5000 and 10,000; and coins are 5, 10, 25, 50 and 100. When it comes to coins, anything below about Rp50 is scarce and for those purchases that cost a couple of hundred dollars, a small wheel barrow may be required! I recommend that travellers use rupiah.

Approximate exchange rates as of October 1994 were:

A$	= Rp1540	Can$	= Rp1560
NZ$	= Rp1250	Sing$	= Rp1100
U.K.L	= Rp 3,270	U.S.A.$	= Rp 2,150

Cash and traveller's cheques are very easy to change in the major centres. Money changers are very competitive in Kuta, Sanur and Ubud, but not in remote areas. Avoid big notes. *Bank Duta* will accept Visa and Mastercard only for cash advances in Denpasar and Kuta.

Banking Hours - Denpasar, Kuta and Sanur the banks are open Mon-Fri, 8.30am to 4.30pm. Money changers - hours vary.

COMMUNICATIONS

Telephones

The telecommunications system has vastly improved in the last couple of years. Telkom is slowly modernising the system and its domestic satellite network now reaches all over Indonesia. These days international operators can be connected in a matter of minutes.

Many phone numbers changed in 1993, increasing most five-digit numbers to six. Should you call an old number a recorded message, in both Indonesian and English, will tell you how to convert the number.

Some useful local numbers: operator 108, overseas operator 102, police 110, complaints 117.

Kantor telekomunikasi (telephone offices), but usually referred to as *wartels*, are operated by Telkom and private enterprise. Local, long-distance and international calls can be made from these offices and they also have **telegram, telex** and **fax** services. A one-minute call to Australia, New Zealand or the US costs about Rp5600. In areas with automatic exchanges, the phone will display the price (and may or may not show the 10% tax); areas without an automatic exchange, calls must be booked for a minimum of three minutes.

Public telephones can be used to make international calls billed to your home phone, but you must have a foreign telephone credit card (purchased in your home country). **Home Country Direct phones (where you connect with your home country operator so that you can pay with a credit card or reverse the charges) are increasing in number.**

Telkom Indonesian telephone cards can be purchased with a face value of 60, 100, 140, 280, 400 or 680 units. The standard cost is Rp82.5 per unit, but some places charge much more than the standard rate. If charged the standard rate, an international call will be about the same price as a call made from a wartel.

Post Offices

For post restante services it is best to use Kuta, Ubud and Sanur. *For incoming mail:* Family Name in Capitals, then *Kantor Pos* and town name. ID and Rp100 is required. Kuta Post Office is at Jl. Raya Tuban and is only open in the mornings. Fax facilities here. **Postal rates** for *postcards* to all international destinations is Rp600. Airmail letters up to 20 grams cost Rp1000 to Australia, Rp1400 to Europe and Rp1600 to the US and Canada.

Newspapers

Bali Post is published fortnightly in English. Three other newspapers in English originate in Jakarta: *The Indonesian Times*, *The Jakarta Post* and *The Indonesian Observer*.

MISCELLANEOUS

Shipping

Items under 10kg can be sent through the post office and can be registered and insured. Customs have to inspect so only wrap after inspection. Customs closes at 1pm so arrive early. Air cargo is charged by the kg. Pt Golden Bali Express, Jl Kartini 52, Denpasar are reputable and efficient.
Metric measurements are used for all weights and measures.

Time

GMT + 8 hours, AEST - 2 hours. As Bali is close to the equator, daylight hours vary only slightly, generally 5am to 5pm.

Electricity

The current is usually 220-240 volts 50 cycles AC and uses a two-pronged plug. Take a torch though, street lighting is poor.

Dress Requirements

Entrance to a temple requires a sarong and sash, though long pants and sash suffice. Sashes are often available for hire. Nude bathing is not appreciated at all and is in fact illegal. Dress sensibly when dealing with banks, consulates, etc. Pack a hat and sunscreen.

Conduct

The carefree attitude of the Balinese belies a strict code of conduct and morals. *Some tips:* Always *remove your shoes* when entering a private residence. The *left hand* is associated with toilet activities so give and receive with the right hand. It is *rude to point* and never, *never pat anyone on the head.* The head is considered to be the seat of the soul. I've also been told it is *rude to blow your nose* in public.

Tipping is not customary but if someone has provided a service it's appreciated.

Mandi and Toilets

Sooner or later you will encounter Indonesian-style bathrooms. The tub filled with water is not a bath. You stand next to the tub and pour water over yourself with the pot. As for the toilets, there are the raised western style affairs and the floor-level, starting-block variety. The locals do not use toilet paper and the toilets are easily blocked. Use the pot to wash down the waste for the starting-block variety.

Health

Pack a small first-aid kit. Cuts and scratches are susceptible to infection in the tropical climate, so wash them quickly and apply an antiseptic. Many travellers complain about "Bali-belly". Do not drink the water. Don't even think of brushing your teeth in it or putting your toothbrush under the tap. Use bottled or boiled water. Stay clear of ice cubes. Avoid seafood in isolated places. If you have tummy problems avoid juice and reduce your food intake, and if it persists see a doctor.

> If you follow all of the above but still drink voluminous quantities of alcohol, avoid sleep, expose yourself to the sun and heat for long periods, and generally indulge yourself to excess — you'll probably develop "Bali-belly" anyway.

Medical Care

Medical assistance is obtainable at any time and most doctors speak English. *Sanglah Public Hospital*, Jl. Kesehatan Selatan 1, Sanglah Denpasar, ph (0361) 227 911. *Wangaya Public Hospital*, Jl. Kartini, Denpasar, ph (0361) 222 141. *Rumah Sakit Umum* (Public Hospital) Jl. Ngurah Rai, Singaraja, ph 41 046.
If you simply need to see a doctor, Kuta Clinic is open 24 hours - Jl. Raya Kuta, Kuta, ph 753 268 or the medical centre at Nusa Dua, ph 71118.
For *emergency dental treatment* see Dr Indra Guizot, Jl. Patimura 19, Denpasar ph (0361) 222 445, 226 445.

Police

Denpasar. Jl. Diponegoro, ph 110.
Kuta. Jl. Raya Kuta, ph 751 598.

Drugs

Once upon a time Bali was a haven for mind-altering substances. Not so now. The drug penalties are extremely harsh and Indonesian gaols are said to be hell! There is no distinction between small and large quantities, and importation and possession are treated the same. In fact, it is an offence not to inform the authorities of offenders.

Photography

Generally, it is advisable to purchase film duty-free before arriving on the island. Slide and print film is easily purchased in the major centres, but buy only the film in airconditioned cases. It is better not to buy camera batteries in Bali so remember to take spares.
In Denpasar, Sanur, Kuta, Ubud and Singaraja there are one-hour developers, and the going rate is around Rp12,000 to develop 36 prints. Given that the standard of developing has

greatly improved and that film does not endure well in the humidity, it is worth having films developed on the island. If you do not have a filter avoid taking photos between about 10am and 2pm as the sun is overhead and photos will have a bluish tinge.

Theft

In the last couple of years, the number of thefts on Bali has increased. Pickpocketing often occurs in crowded places and the locals, even though embarrassed by the incident, will not tell tourists their wallet is being lifted. The most prevalent type of theft is usually by deceit. Guys, but sometimes girls, will devise an elaborate story about a poor family member, etc, which usually results in the victim handling over large wads of money. Beware of rush tactics (many tourists are duped by the sense of urgency) and never ever accept an invitation to see someone's village. Offers of assistance, be it for a car, camera, etc, will usually be very costly.

Travel Insurance

A must. But read the fine print. The medical facilities for emergencies are restricted so make sure your policy has provisions for your safe and swift removal from the island.

Churches

Churches belonging to christian denominations are present on the island. **Roman Catholic:** *St Francis Xavier, Tuban, Kuta. Jl. Kepurdung, Denpasar. Mass - Sunday 8.00am.* **Grand Bali Beach Hotel, Sanur, Legong Room, Saturday 5pm,** *Bali Hyatt Hotel, Sanur, Hibiscus Room, Saturday 6pm,* **Bali Sol Hotel, Nusa Dua Conference Hall, Sunday 5pm,** *Nusa Dua Beach Hotel, Sunday 6.00pm.* **Pentecostal:** *Jl. Karna, Denpasar.***Protestant Church:** Maranatha, Jl. Surapati, Jl. Debes, and Jl. Ngurah Rai, Singaraja. Service Hotel Bali Beach, Sunday 6pm. *Evangelical Church:* Jl. Melati Denpasar.

TRAVEL INFORMATION

HOW TO GET THERE

By Air

Cathay Pacific fly direct to Denpasar Mon, Fri, Sat from Hong Kong.

Continental has flights to Denpasar from:
Los Angeles, San Francisco via Honolulu and Guam (the hub)
Tues, Wed, Fri, Sat.

Ansett has flights to Denpasar from:

Sydney -	Wed and Sat
Melbourne -	Sat and Sun
Perth -	Sat and Sun
Darwin -	Wed and Sat

Qantas has flights to Denpasar from:

Sydney -	Sat and Sun direct
Melbourne -	Tues, Thurs and Sun
Perth -	Sat and Sun direct
San Francisco -	Mon, Fri, Sat via Sydney
Los Angeles -	Mon, Tues, Sat via Sydney
Auckland -	Tues, Wed, Sun via Sydney
London via Perth -	Thurs, Sat

Singapore Airlines flies to Denpasar daily from Singapore and from London via Singapore.

Garuda Indonesia is the national carrier and has flights to Denpasar from:

Sydney -	daily except Thursday

Melbourne -	daily except Thursday
Perth -	daily except Monday
Adelaide -	Mon and Fri
Brisbane -	Mon and Fri
Darwin -	Tues and Sat
Auckland -	Tues and Sat
London -	Mon, Wed and Sat
Singapore -	daily
Hong Kong -	daily
Honolulu -	Tues, Wed, Fri Sat via Biak

Los Angeles - Mon, Wed, Thurs, Sat, via Honolulu and Biak.

From Java

By Train

It is possible to begin the trip to Bali by train from Surabaya. The best way to make the 16-hour trip to Surabaya from Jakarta is by the first-class airconditioned *Mutiara Utara* night express train, which costs about US$33 one-way. There are also   second and third class trains available that are much cheaper, but they take so long they're not really an option.

From Gubeng Station in Surabaya, take the *Mutiara Timur* train, which departs at 11am and 9.30pm for Banyuwangi on the eastern tip of Java. Unfortunately, it takes about eight hours and is not airconditioned, but it only costs about US$4. Then you transfer to a bus which takes the ferry across to Bali and continues on to Denpasar, all for US$1.

By Bus

There are regular bus services from Jakarta to Bali, obviously also including a ferry jaunt, and the trip takes about 30 hours. Buses leave from Pulo Gadung Terminal in the early morning and late afternoon, and the fare is about US$20.

There is also a service from Yogya to Bali, which takes about 16 hours and costs US$10, with numerous departures daily. And an airconditioned service from Surabaya to Denpasar costs about US$8, and takes ten to 12 hours. Some buses will travel on to Kuta and Sanur, if yours doesn't, it is very easy to catch a taxi or charter a bemo.

Agents in Jakarta can provide bus tickets, and your hotel can supply information on the closest one.

By Ferry
Any form of transport from Java to Bali has, of course, to link up with the ferry. The journey across the strait takes about 25 minutes and private and government ferries ply the route, leaving at 15 to 20-minute intervals. But if it's vacation time, waiting to board can take hours.
From Bali you can trip across to the island of Lombok from Padangbai on the east coast. The ferry departs at 10am and 2pm and costs about US$3-$4.

TOURIST INFORMATION
There is a tourist information centre at the airport, but it is recommended that you visit the offices in Denpasar or Kuta.

The head office of the Bali Government Tourism Office is located on Jl. Raya Puputan, Niti Mandala, Renon, Denpasar. There are also branch offices on the island and information on these is included in the section pertaining to each area.

ACCOMMODATION
Bali offers a wide range of accommodation from opulent 5 star hotels to spartan *losmen*. Prices vary according to location, availability of airconditioning and hot water, as well as season. It is wise to book early during December to February.

I have listed a range of hotels in the sections on the various towns, but please remember that the prices quoted should be used as a guide only. Rates can change quickly, although you can probably be sure they won't be reduced.

Another thing. Many hotels call themselves "cottages" and "bungalows", when in reality they are two-storey cement blocks.

LOCAL TRANSPORT

Taxis

Taxis are available in Denpasar, Kuta and the airport, and fares are fixed. Generally taxis charge Rp800 flagfall and Rp800 per kilometre. At Ngurah Rai Airport a ticket can be purchased from the desk outside customs.

Public Bemos

The most convenient and cheapest form of transport is the public bemo. However, this form of transport is not to be confused with bemos available for charter — they're a different story. Public bemos are especially handy for travelling between Denpasar and Kuta, Denpasar and Ubud, and Kuta and Sanur.

Public bemos operate from dawn to dusk, and although they don't operate to a timetable they are frequent. The fares are fixed, but unfortunately tourist prices are gaining favour, so they may vary for different bemos. You can often ask the going rate but sometimes the locals clam-up and you may have to bargain with the fare collector. For public bemo terminals, see the entries in the sections on the various towns.

Private Bemos

The all-pervading bemos for charter soon become pestilent. Forever soliciting, they seem to have little success. Although they bargain, they demand exorbitant prices and unless you're desperate for a ride, an encounter with these people is simply an exercise in exasperation. If you're travelling in a group a shared fare may not be so painful, and they are convenient for travelling to outlying attractions.

Dokars

Dokars are pony-driven carts, and during Dutch colonisation Dokars were the most luxurious means of transportation.

Now they have been superseded by machines but they are still to be found in poorer places and, of course, there are a few for the pleasure of travellers.

Do-it-yourself

Driving around Bali is the best way to see the island. Having said that, a word of warning. It's not so much that the Balinese drive fast — in fact they travel on average at about 40kph. They're not maniacal, impatient, rude or tense. It's more the overcrowding. The roads are often narrow and pot-holed, and a lot of bicycles and motorbikes use them. In fact, trying to pass motorbikes five-abreast, with families precariously perched on them (women side-saddle) can be a little disconcerting. Not to mention contending with stray dogs, cats and chickens which may feel compelled to amble across the road with little fear of their impending peril. There are road rules: always honk before overtaking (most motorbikes don't have mirrors) and the bigger the vehicle, the more right of way. Good luck!

The authorities do not issue temporary licences so you must be in possession of an international driver's licence. There are few petrol stations so keep an eye on the fuel gauge. The station on Jl. Puputan in Denpasar is open 24 hours.

Car rentals

If you do decide to drive, the Suzuki Jimny, which costs around $30 a day, is popular. Prices are fixed, but bargaining is permissible for longer periods. Scrutinise the vehicle before you pay for it, and then get yourself to the nearest petrol station — there'll be just enough petrol to get you there.

Here are some addresses of rental agents:
Avis Rent-A-Car, Jl. Veteran 5, Denpasar, ph 224 233; Jl. Raya Kuta, *Kuta*, ph 751 474; Bali Hyatt Hotel, Sanur, ph 88 271.
Bali Beringin Car Rental, Jl. Raya Airport 2, ph 751 356.
Bali Car Rental, Jl. By-pass Ngurah Rai, Sanur, ph 88 550/359.
Giri Putra Car Rental, Jl. Raya Kuta 504, Kuta, ph 751 349.

Motorbike rentals

Motorbike casualties, particularly tourist casualties, occur with monotonous regularity.

Make sure you are insured for accidents and that you are covered for emergency transportation back home.

* Shop around for the best deal, remembering that safety is of the utmost importance - consider the state of the motorbike.

* Always carry the registration papers with you.

* If you really intend to travel by motorbike take your own helmet because the plastic affairs that accompany the bike are about as protective as a paper bag.

* And don't make the mistake of leaving your passport with the rental agent - don't laugh, it happens too often.

* You should possess an international motorbike licence, if not, you can spend four hours at the police station in Denpasar going through the rigmarole of being tested. Licences are not difficult to procure, but be patient and dress respectably.

Bicycles

Cycling is yet another form of transport on this wonderful island. There are plenty of bikes to hire at very reasonable prices, but make sure that the bike is roadworthy.

Tip

For serious bikers: don't ride at night or the middle of the day; take plenty of water; and wear a hat.

The following table gives some idea of the distances involved in touring Bali.

Distances from Denpasar to -	
Amlapura -	78km (48 miles)
Bangli -	**40km (25 miles)**
Batubulan -	8km (5 miles)
Bedugul -	**46km (29 miles)**
Besakih -	61km (38 miles)
Celuk -	**11km (7 miles)**
Gelgel -	43km (27 miles)
Gianyar -	**27km (17 miles)**
Gilimanuk -	128km (80 miles)
Kintamani -	**68km (42 miles)**
Klungkung -	40km (25 miles)
Kuta -	**9km (6 miles)**
Mas -	22km (14 miles)
Negara -	**95km (59 miles)**
Nusa Dua -	23km (14 miles)
Sanur -	**7km (4 miles)**
Singaraja -	78km (48 miles)
Tampaksiring -	**37km (23 miles)**
Tanah Lot -	31km (19 miles)
Ubud -	**25km (16 miles)**
Ulu Watu -	30km (19 miles)

DAY TOURS

Most hotels offer day tours, as do the numerous tour agents. The island is so small that it's possible to travel from say, Kuta in the south, to Singaraja on the north coast, in about three hours. So even if you plant yourself in one place it is still possible to cover all of Bali.

For tours with a difference, try sailing around Bali in crystal-clear waters. Book a day trip, or groups can charter a yacht for extended trips to other islands in the archipelago. *Trade Wind Yacht Charter* (PT Tourdevco) is highly recommended, and can be located at Bali Benoa Port (from overseas), ph 62 361, 31591, fax 62 361, 31592, PO Box 1081, Tuban, Denpasar, Bali, Indonesia.

Sightseeing attractions and suggested tours are listed in each section.

FOOD AND DRINK

Balinese daily fare is simple. Most meals are created around white rice or *nasi*, and there is little variation. Brightly coloured rice cakes (*jaja*) are the usual Balinese breakfast, and other meals involve rice mixed with vegetables, peanuts and sometimes meat (beef being the exception). Spices, especially chilli, are sprinkled with gay abandon.

There are no real meal times. Women prepare and cook the food in the morning, leaving it in pots covered with palm leaves, for leisurely consumption throughout the day. It seems that eating is one of the few activities the Balinese choose to do alone.

Festive Foods

Feasts for the gods are a different matter. Ceremonial food is a community effort focused in the kitchen of the temple. The men usually slaughter the animals in the early hours of the morning, and then cook the meat in the temple, and the women tend to the rice and vegetable dishes. When the preparation is complete, the food is divided and some laid on banana-leaf squares as offerings to the gods, the leftovers are for the cooks.

A feast might entail *babi guling* (roasted suckling pig), *betutu bebek* (duckling roasted in banana leaf), *nasi goreng* (fried rice mixed with meat and vegetables), perhaps *mei goreng* (fried noodles) and definitely *lawar* (a salad of finely shredded meats, coconut, papaya and spices). Of course, no banquet would be complete without a sate, usually chicken (*ayam*), pork (*babi*), beef or turtle meat, which are skewered and smothered in a peanut sauce. *Rijstaffel*, the much-lauded

Dutch "rice table" creation, is a variety of side dishes served with steamed rice.

Popular dishes of the archipelago include *soto ayam* (chicken broth), *ikan* (fish) cooked in various spices and sauces, *nasi padang* a very spicy but cold Sumatran dish, and *gado-gado* (rice salad with peanut sauce).

Meals are accompanied by *sambal* sauce, a concoction of shallots, turmeric, ginger, garlic, cardamom seeds and red peppers. It's hot!

Restaurants

In the tourist triangle, there is a multitude of restaurants specialising in a multitude of cuisines. Indonesian food is common, but real Balinese food is rare, and both are modified for Western tastebuds. If you really want to sample genuine Balinese food, go no further than the various night markets (*pasar malam*).

The street stalls, called *warung*, also offer authentic Indonesian and Balinese food. Like restaurants, the more clientele, the better the quality of food — well, in theory anyway.

Drinks

In the tropics, cold drinks take on a whole new meaning. Every restaurant, *warung* and bar serves iced juice: any fruit you'd care to mention is blended with ice, and sometimes coconut milk. The addition of avocado makes this already luscious drink, nectar for the gods.

Water, tea and coffee are all consumed in copious amounts on a daily basis, but the Balinese have also created some wicked brews. The distinctive Balinese drink, *brem*, is a sweet, red rice-wine, distilled from red or white sticky rice. Yeast is added to cooked rice which is wrapped, and after a week, wine can be squeezed from the rice. *Tuak* is a mild beer made from the juice of palm flowers, and takes about a day to ferment. The colourless *arak* is distilled from palm or rice wine and has an obnoxious smell. An acquired taste (although it may take only one or two drinks to acquire), it is often consumed straight or with soft drink. Actually, *brem* mixed with *arak* isn't a bad drop.

Beer drinkers will feel at home in Bali. However, as for wine, most of the larger hotels sell imported wines but the prices may be prohibitive.

Fruit

Balinese fruit is a real treat. Pineapples, papaya, coconuts, bananas, mangoes and avocados are plentiful and cheap. But there are some taste sensations that you may not have encountered.

Rambutan - tastes like a cross between a lychee and a grape, and has an unmistakably hairy, red skin. This is definitely my favourite.
Mangosteen - white, segmented flesh, with a purple, black or brown skin. Tastes exquisitely sweet.
Salak - has a hard almost spiky skin with the flesh also hard, and tastes slightly bitter.
Blimbing - has green or yellow skin and its cross-section is star-shaped.
Durian - do not let the odious smell of this fruit deter you. It tastes wonderful.
Nangka - jackfruit.

And of course there's always fresh, icy cold fruit juice.

Coconut Palms

The coconut is revered by the Balinese, probably because every inch of the plant can be used for something. The coconut palm provides: oil for cooking and lamps; sweet water for drinking; the flesh makes milk for cooking; the wood is used for building and furniture; the leaves wrap offerings for the gods; the "palm cabbage" and flesh of the coconut are edible; and the gum from the flower buds is used for palm beer. Copra, the dried flesh from the nut, is exported.

ENTERTAINMENT

There is no shortage of entertainment on Bali. Local dance, puppet and theatre performances provide amusement for those who desire cultural titillation, while at the other end of the spectrum, pubs, bars and discos cater to those who seek less cerebral pleasures.

SHOPPING

Bargaining

If you've come to shop, you've come to the right place. In Bali, the simple "tagged-item-hand-your-money-over" syndrome, is only half the story. There are other approaches you may not have encountered.

There's the highly animated and sometimes anxiety-provoking form of shopping, called bargaining. This is the traditional means of purchasing items and it's expected.

> The secret is: be as humorous, and as theatrical, as the vendor. It's the spirit of the transaction that counts. (It's often a good idea to chant this quietly in moments of frustration.) If you have an idea about how much you'd like to spend, halve it, and name your price. It can't be your final price — the vendor must have room to move — or you will have broken the rules and offended the seller.

Alternatively, ask the price and then make a counter offer much cheaper than you want. Once you have agreed you cannot renege. Sounds easy huh?

Prices will vary according to the season, the seller's profit margin for the day, and her or his estimation of the buyer. And the theory is, the more you buy at the one shop, the better the bargains should be. It's simple. If it's any consolation, everyone feels cheated at least once — put it down to experience. The most important fact is that you bought something you wanted.

Just when you think you've adapted to bargaining, they spring fixed prices on you. There are places where bargaining is inappropriate, for instance, most hotels, shopping centres, supermarkets and restaurants have fixed prices. But when it comes to *losmen*-style accommodation bargaining can be appropriate if you want to stay for a week or if it's the off-peak season (April to October). Many boutiques and jewellery shops have fixed prices but are very competitive, especially in the south.

And then there's the "don't-come-to-us, we'll-come-to-you" brigade. On the beach, walking down the street, sometimes even in the hotel grounds, are hawkers importuning you to buy, buy, buy, and most of the stuff simply isn't worth buying. Massages are a different story. For around US$3 you can indulge yourself with the blessed hands of these experts. If you should return the following day, the same masseur will provide a longer massage for the same price.

> If intending to shop while on a guided tour, the guide will receive a percentage of your purchases, which will be reflected in the final price. This is standard practice and reflected in their wages.

Batik and Other Fabrics

Surprisingly, the majority of *batik* is machine-made and imported from Java. Nonetheless, exquisite hand-made *batik* can be found in the village of Gianyar. Traditional Balinese hand-woven fabrics are probably the best buys, and can be purchased in shops in Gianyar and Singaraja.

In Singaraja (on Jl. Veteran in between the library and tourist information service) is Puri Agung Sinar Nadi where women weave silken fabrics on the premises.

In Tenganan (about a kilometre out of Candi Dasa proper), women still practise the art of double *ikat*, which involves tie-dyeing both the weft and warp threads before weaving. Known as *geringsing*, the cloth is quite expensive but very, very elegant.

Leather Goods

Kuta is the best place to buy leather. The shops are very competitive and the goods are more fashionable than in the other tourist centres. In most places the price is negotiable, but fixed-prices are gaining popularity. Like any other purchase, shop around and assess the market.

Leather jackets are made to order, but it's advisable to ascertain your correct measurements from a jacket that fits, before you leave home. For instance, arm length, shoulder width, wrist, shoulder to waist, and waist measurements are good figures to take with you. Some people have walked out of leather shops less than impressed with their purchases.

Paintings

Ubud is the place to buy paintings.

Visit the **Neka Gallery** and the **Puri Lukisan Museum,** both in Ubud, to familiarise yourself with the different styles. You'll find the staff at both places very helpful, and they will divulge information on different styles, quality and prices. The nearby villages of Pengosekan and Peliatan have communities of artists famed for their distinctive styles. Batuan (on the road to Ubud or Gianyar) is well-known for black and white ink paintings and the sombre, dark Batuan style of painting.

Silver

The best place to purchase silver is **Celuk.** The silver jewellery made there is of filigree design and is usually about 90% silver; and you can even see the silversmiths practising their art. Beratan, a village on the outskirts of Singaraja, is also known for the "dynamic Buleleng" style of silversmithing.

Unfortunately, silver tarnishes in high humidity, especially on perspiring skin, so it's an idea not to wear it until you return home. Also, don't clean the silver in the various dips available, because it removes the protective oxidised coating, making it tarnish permanently.

Turtle Products

In the markets of Kuta and Sanur there are numerous turtle products for sale, including jewellery, carvings, tacky lacquered turtle shells, etc. The World Wildlife Fund has urged the government to cease the trade as the turtles are fast becoming an endangered species. Anyway, anyone attempting to import turtle products into most western countries will have them confiscated by customs.

Woodcarving

Mas is probably the best place to window shop, but the best place to buy woodcarvings is Batuan. Prices differ as to the intricacy of the carving and quality of the wood. There are many types of wood, from the indigenous "white" jackwood and mottled coconut, to the imported teak and ebony. But be careful, your beautiful ebony statue might just be painted jackwood.

RECREATION

Golf

The Natour Grand Bali Beach in Sanur (ph 288 271), has a nine-hole course. Real enthusiasts need look no further than the Bali Handara Golf Club, in the regency of Buleleng. It is said to be the best course in Asia and one of the most beautiful in the world.

Surfing

by Mark Naylor

Bali really is a surfer's dream come true. Mainly because it's cheap, accessible, tropical, has perfect coral reefs and beach breaks, and has consistent large and powerful swells coinciding with favourable trade winds.

Bali's most consistent surf (and its driest months) coincides with the Southern Hemisphere's winter months, June to August. By the same token, Bali receives good waves all year round.

Bali has two main surf seasons:

1. By far the surfers' most popular is the dry season, from late March through to September or October.

This is dictated by wind direction and the fact that large swells are generated in the southern Indian Ocean by severe storms at this time of the year.

Wind direction then means the best surf is on the Kuta side of the island, including the reef breaks such as *Kuta reef, Ulu Watu, Padang Padang and Bingen*. These breaks are all world-class waves breaking on shallow coral, and are recommended for experienced surfers only. This coral is razor sharp and any cuts received will quickly become infected, so a first-aid kit is a must!

For surfers of a lesser standard

Kuta Beach, Legian Beach, Canggu and many lesser-known spots are recommended.

A word of warning: these beaches still receive large swells and can be very dangerous. **It is possible to rent surfboards at Kuta Beach.**

2. From October to late February is Bali's wet season and there is a change of wind direction.

This means the trade winds favour the Sanur side of the island. Swells during these months can be large, and sometimes wild and out of control, being generated by

In between these storms, perfect waves can be found at places such as Nusa Dua and Mushroom Rock, and Sanur itself can be one of the best waves on the island. **All these breaks are coral based** — there are no beach breaks on this side of the island (that I know of, anyway).

Although it may be the wet, humid, and sometimes unbearable time of the year, it can pay dividends as far as being less crowded and it is possible to surf the lesser-known reef breaks (of which there are many).

Boardriders making their way to the point at Nusa Dua

Other Islands

Nusa Lembongon is the closest island to Bali being only a few hours' boat ride.

A great escape to some great waves. Some high quality reef breaks include "shipwreck" and "lacerations".

These are the two most popular breaks, and both can be terrifyingly shallow, and crowded, due to lack of easily accessible breaks. There are a few secret spots on the island reached by a short boat ride.

There are numerous surf shops in Kuta and Legian, but Lili's Surf Shop, on the north side of Jl. Legian in Kuta, is owned by Gede Narmada, one of Bali's best surfers. When he's not surfing, he is very willing to talk surf.

Diving and Snorkelling

Bali's underwater world is stunning. Surrounded by coral reefs, the island has warm, clear waters. The areas of Nusa Dua, Sanur, Tulamben, Menjangan Island, Lembongan and Nusa Penida are frequently visited by divers. Whether you're experienced, a novice, or simply want to sit in a glass-bottomed boat, the sights are not to be missed.

A couple of places recommended for hiring equipment are:

Bali Marine Sports Dive Centre, Jl. By-pass Ngurah Rai, Sanur, ph 87 872.

Wisata Tirtha Alpha, Jl. Pratama Tanjung Benoa, Nusa Dua, ph 72 116.

Water Skiing and Parasailing

Lake Bratan, in Bedugul, has become the water skiing capital of Bali. Boats, skis and ramps are available from the Bedugul Hotel in the arcade on the shores of the lake.

In Sanur, waterskiing equipment is available from Bali Marine Sports, on the beach, south of the Bali Hyatt. The centre also offers parasailing, as do the hotels at Nusa Dua.

BADUNG

The regency of Badung is the most populated area in Bali, and encompasses the capital city, Denpasar, and the tourist triangle of Kuta, Sanur and Nusa Dua. A narrow strip of land, Badung extends north to the slopes of Gunung Batur and south to the tip of the Bukit Peninsula.

Badung is blessed with fine rivers and fertile volcanic soils. Of course, the Balinese themselves have dauntlessly nurtured a complex irrigation network, and meticulously utilised every inch of land to yield their crops. But far from being simply an agrarian land, Badung is also favoured with white beaches, stunning postcard-like sunsets, and a developed tourist trade. Maybe the gods are crazy!

By sea, it is the most accessible area in the south, and since the 1920s, when Mads Lang established his post at Kuta, Badung has steadily been influenced by Java and the West. But it wasn't until the international airport was built at Tuban in 1969, that the regency really expanded. Since then, the government has seen that tourism remains centred in Badung, so the south has experienced whirlwind changes ahead of the rest of the island.

HISTORY

Badung has had a rather short, but nevertheless illustrious, history. The earliest known example of writing was discovered at Belanjong, near Sanur, and it suggests that Hinduism had reached Badung by 914AD. Badung, however, did not enter the limelight until the late 19th century. The Pemecutan family, Badung's ruling clan, subjugated the princes of Mengwi, the neighbouring regency, in 1891, and

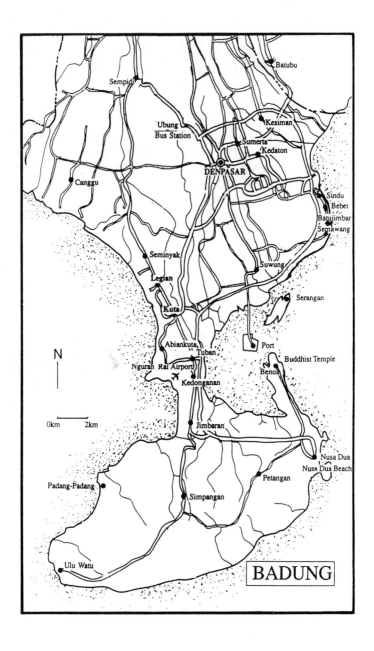

BADUNG

Badung became a powerful force. But the Dutch had conquered the north and the west by the mid 19th century, and were waiting for an opportunity to take the south. They didn't have to wait long.

The Balinese had taken to plundering trade ships that foundered on the surrounding reefs, and the Dutch used this as a pretext to intervene. In 1906, the Dutch landed at Sanur and marched to Badung (present-day Denpasar) where they were met by the Raja of Pemecutan and thousands of resolute Balinese adorned in cremation attire. Rather than surrender, the Balinese chose suicide: *puputan*. It wasn't the first *puputan*, nor the last, but it was certainly the demise of the royalty in south Bali.

DENPASAR

In 1958, Denpasar emerged phoenix-like as the capital of Bali.

Pasar means "market" and that's what Denpasar is: a congested, noisy, dusty market. But a burgeoning market at that, where old is pitted against new. Western-style concrete buildings dwarf classical Balinese architecture. Satellite disks dot the skyline. Bemos, motorbikes and carts vie for space on narrow streets originally built for horse-driven dokars. Dust, smoke and fumes, not to mention the cacophony of horns, brakes and people, blend to create a vexing atmosphere. Denpasar is the antithesis of most people's expectations of Bali.

Look at it this way. The Balinese seek to achieve a balance between opposites, and anything less than a balance means chaos, and possibly destruction. If Bali is as paradisiacal as many people claim, something had to be diametrically opposed. And Denpasar, with all the charm of a dump, is it.

Denpasar, market cum city, is one of the richest places in Indonesia. Many say that it's a small-scale replica of Jakarta, and that the youth of the city look to the Indonesian capital for inspiration. The national language, Bahasa Indonesia, is

· spoken almost to the exclusion of Balinese dialects, and the educated Hindus preach of one supreme God, reconciling their beliefs with the creeds of a united Indonesia (*pancasila*).

Getting Your Bearings

The main street, *Gaja Mada*, runs from east to west, and is lined with shops, restaurants and small businesses. *Jalan Veteran*, the other main street, intersects with *Gaja Mada* at the statute of Batara Guru (the Lord Teacher). The field across from the statute is Puputan Square.

Some Words of Advice

Denpasar is not a place for tourists to stay. Spend the day looking around, but a day in Denpasar can be enough for a lifetime.

For those travelling to Denpasar by bemo: beware! When disembarking, young people will greet you and offer their services as guides. Ignore them at all costs, despite their persistence. They're working for shop-owners who pay them a percentage and they'll escort you to somewhere that has "very good prices", but upon arrival vendors will descend like carrion and you'll feel compelled to buy just to escape.

HOW TO GET THERE

By Public Bemo

From Ngurah Rai Airport, bemos depart from the main road, not far from the gates of the airport, and cost about Rp800.

In Kuta, bemos leave from the famed Bemo Corner very frequently and the fare is Rp500.

By Hiring a Bemo

From the airport, bemos can be chartered for Rp10,000. Bemos are no longer permitted to park in the airport carpark, but that hasn't stopped them. Personally, I'd rather negotiate with a tribe of people-eaters, and would recommend a taxi.

By Taxi

From the airport, a ticket can be purchased at the taxi stand outside customs. Taxis have fixed prices from Kuta to Denpasar and cost around Rp9000. Generally taxis charge Rp800 for flagfall and Rp800 per kilometre.

By Car

Denpasar is 9km (6 miles) from Kuta and the drive takes about half an hour. See the "travel information" section for distances.

TOURIST INFORMATION

The head office of the Bali Government Tourism Office is at Jl. Raya Puputan, Niti Mandala, Renon, Denpasar, opposite Puputan Square. The tourist office that serves the regency of Badung is on Jl. Surapati, Denpasar, ph 223 602.

Both offices provide a map and information on monthly activities and festivals.

ACCOMMODATION

There is no shortage of accommodation in Denpasar, but only the Indonesians or business people stay here for the night.

Prices are in US$ for one night's accommodation and should be used as a guide only. **The telephone code is 0361**.

Natour Bali Hotel, Jl. Veteran 3, ph 225 681. Room $60-$90.

Hotel Denpasar, Jl. Diponegoro 103, ph 226 363. Room $25-$35.

Pemecutan Palace, Jl. Thamrin 2, ph 223 491. Room $35.

Tohpati Bali Hotel, Jl. By-pass Ngurah Rai 15, ph 235 408. Suite $176.

Adi Yasa, Jl. Nakula 23B, ph 222 679. Pleasant and well-kept. Room Rp8000-Rp12,000.

Bali International Youth Hostel, Jl. Mertesari Desar Sidakarya. Newly opened.

LOCAL TRANSPORT

Negotiating Denpasar on foot is probably the easiest way to see the place, then you don't have to worry about traffic jams, parking, or the one-way streets.

By Public Bemo

As Denpasar is "bemo central", it's the best place to find public transport to just about anywhere on the island. Bemos also run between terminals and the fare is Rp500.

The four main terminals are:

Tegel station is south of the city on the road to Kuta and provides services to the south of Bali including all other terminals in Denpasar:

Airport	Rp800
Kuta	Rp500
Legian	Rp600
Sanur	Rp600
Nusa Dua	Rp1000

Ubung terminal is north of the centre and provides services to the north:

Kediri	Rp1000
Mengwi	Rp1000
Negara	Rp3500
Gilimanuk	Rp4500
Bedugul	Rp1800
Singaraja	Rp2000

Kerengeng terminal, to the east, is mainly for services in Denpasar, but also has a direct bemo service to Sanur (Rp500).

Batubulan terminal runs services for eastern and central Bali:

Ubud	Rp1000
Gianyar	Rp1000
Tampaksiring	Rp1200
Klungkung	Rp1200

Bangli	Rp1200
Padangbai	Rp2000
Candi Dasa	Rp2200
Amlapura	Rp3000
Kintamani	Rp2000

EATING OUT
Denpasar has the widest selection of Chinese restaurants on the island, but for Indonesian food try the night markets.

Restaurants
Akasaka Restaurant, Jl. Teuku Umar Simpang 6.
Good Japanese food.
Atoom Baru, Jl. Gaja Mada 106. International selection, but specialises in Chinese food.
Hong Kong International, Jl. Gaja Mada 85.
Kak Man, Jl. Teuka Umar. Specialises in traditional Balinese food, and for this reason alone should not be overlooked.
Melati Indah, Jl. Diponegoro 46.
Minang Indah, Jl. Diponegoro 35.
Natour Bali Hotel, Jl. Veteran. Specialises in Dutch East Indies-style food and they make a great *rijstaffel* (a Dutch hotch-potch of Indonesian foods).
Puri Selera Restaurant, JL. Gaja Mada. Good Chinese food.
Restaurant Betty, Jl. Sumatra 56.
Simpang Enam Restaurant, Jl. Teuka Umar. Serves some wonderful traditional Indonesian meals.

Night Markets
The night markets or *pasar malam* are invariably cheap and good, and as the Indonesians and Balinese frequent the markets you can be assured of sumptuous delights.
Kerengeng, at the bemo station of the same name, opens around 5pm and has a wide range of Indonesian and Balinese.
Kumbasari, in the Kumbasari market complex, is small but there are some good Chinese food stalls.

Tiara Dewata Food Centre, in the complex of the same name, is the biggest market, with a large range of Indonesian fare.

ENTERTAINMENT

Sadly, most of the dance performances in Denpasar are mediocre. STSI (the College of Indonesian Arts, see below) is recommended, but Ubud really is the place to be captivated by some of the best dancers on the island.

Kecak dance, Ayodya Pura Stage, Tanjung Bungkak, 6.30-8.30pm; or at the Werdhi Budaya Art Centre, Jl. Nusa Indah, 6.30-8.30pm.

Barong leak, Taman Budaya, Denpasar - daily 9.30-10.30am.

The College of Indonesian Arts (STSI), Jl. Nusa Inda (near the arts centre). Anytime during the morning you can marvel at student dancers and musicians practising traditional and modern performances.

SHOPPING

As mentioned previously, "pasar" means market and Denpasar's full of them. The Kumbasari Market, on the east bank of the Badung river (in the middle of the city) is a huge concrete building crammed with three floors of vendors: fruit and vegetables on the ground floor, household goods on the second, and clothes on the third.

Antiques

You'll really have to scrutinise the merchandise or you may have purchased a genuine fake.

The Arts of Asia Gallery. Tucked behind a shopping centre (Jl. Thamrin 27, Block C5), is one of the best-known antique shops in Bali, and the proprietor, Verra Darwiko, is very knowledgeable.

Books

Corsica Books, Jl. Sumatra. This bookshop has a good selection of books on Bali.

Coffee

Not surprisingly, Bali produces some fine coffees. Toko *Bhineka Jaya*, on Jl. Gaja Mada has a wondrous array of coffees to satisfy the most discerning of coffee connoisseurs.

Electronics

Few people realise that electronic goods in Denpasar are quite cheap. Here's a list of some of the shops:

Denpasar Electronic, Jl. Veteran 25, ph 227 479.

Palapa Agung Electronic, Jl. Sumatra 8, ph 225 721.

Surya, Jl. Gaja Mada 128, ph 222 254.

Toyobo Electronic, Jl. Diponegoro, ph 222 613.

Gold

Despite the claims of the jewellers from Celuk, Denpasar is the best place to buy gold, and there are quite a few gold shops in Denpasar. Just take a stroll down Jl. Sulawesi and Jl. Hasanuddin. Most of the gold is 22kt and is sold by weight. **The prices are often comparable with those in Singapore and Hong Kong.**

Textiles

Denpasar has many fabric shops, particularly along Jl. Sulawesi, or you can venture into the *Kumbasari Market* (third floor).

Dua Lima and *Toko Murah*, both on Jl. Sulawesi, are reputable fabric shops.

Pertenuan AAA on Jl. Veteran (near the Bali Hotel) is one of the larger weaving factories in Bali, and sells the renowned tie-dyed *endek*.

After you've purchased some fine cloth, have it transformed into clothes by the following dressmakers:

Sara Burdamas. Jl. Teuku Umar 150, ph 223 267.

Toko Alus. Jl. Gaja Mada 77, ph 224 522.

SIGHTSEEING

The striking thing about Denpasar is the old juxtaposed with the new. Change in Bali has accelerated since the 1970s and Denpasar is where it's happening.

Pura Moaspahit

In the city proper, the most ancient of Denpasar's temples is the Pura Moaspahit. Located in a small alley off Jl. Tabanan, the Pura is guarded by two massive statues: Batara Bayu, the god of wind; and Garuda, messenger of the gods. On the facade are the gods Yama and Indra. The red-brick temple is testimony to the influence of the Majapahit dynasty.

Puri Pemecutan

Just near the central bus station on the corner of Jl. Thamrin and Jl. Hasanudin stands Puri Pemecutan. Once the site of the royal palace for the Pemecutan Empire, it was rebuilt in 1907 as a hotel, after the original palace was destroyed in the 1906 *puputan*. The design emulates the palaces of the former Badung kingdom, and the palace houses *lontar* manuscripts of traditional literature as well as a fine collection of paintings.

Catuh Mukha Statue

The statue which glares in four directions, is at Denpasar's main intersection (corner of Jl. Gaja Mada and Jl. Veteran), and represents the god Bhatara Guru (Siwa). Built in 1972, it was a somewhat belated erection to commemorate the *puputan* of 1906.

Puputan Square

The rather large expanse of lawn in the town is Puputan Square. The statue in the corner is a monument to the heroic men, women and children who sacrificed their lives rather than succumb to the invasion of the Dutch militia in 1906.

Museum Bali

On the eastern side of Puputan Square is the Museum Bali. Erected in 1932 by the Dutch, with the assistance of Walter Spies, it attempted to display the historical and cultural artefacts of Bali within an architectural framework.

Housed in Tabanan, Karangasem and Badung styles of architecture, the museum illustrates the two types of construction in Bali: temples and palaces. The split gate, outer and inner courtyards, and kulkul drum typify the temple. The main building, with its pillared verandah, exemplifies the Karangasem style of architecture. The windowless building on the right resembles the Tabanan style of construction, while the building on the left portrays the style of Badung.

The museum's contents are, unfortunately, a little disappointing. Items range from Neolithic stone implements to modern ceremonial masks and paintings, but they are poorly labelled and rather haphazardly arranged. Nonetheless, the museum is worth visiting simply for the examples of architecture, and it does give the visitor an idea of the history and culture of the island.

The museum is open:
Tuesday to Thursday 7.30am-1.30pm.
Friday 7.30am-11.30am.
Saturday to Sunday 8am - 12pm.
Closed Monday. Admission Rp200.

Pura Jagatnatha

Next to the museum is the relatively new state temple, Pura Jagatnatha. A "world" temple, it's dedicated to Sanghyang Widi, the supreme God. The idea of one supreme god marks a shift in the philosophy of Hindu intellectuals from a polytheistic to a monotheistic religion. The intellectuals have their eyes cast towards Jakarta, so it's said, and reconcile their Hindu beliefs with those of a predominantly Muslim Indonesia. Hence, most gods are manifestations of the Supreme God.

Surrounded by high walls with several entrances, the temple is one of the busiest in Bali. Unfortunately, the temple is closed to the public except for festivals, and even then, locals seem reluctant to welcome foreigners. A strict dress code is enforced, so don't expect to go in without a sarong and sash, and shoulders should be covered. Opposite Pura Jagatnatha is the new military headquarters. You'll probably see some of the militia wandering around town.

Werdhi Budaya Art Centre

Located in the complex on Jl. Nusa Indah, the art centre was built in 1973, and the permanent exhibition is one of the best in Bali.

The Walter Spies Art Gallery in the centre has some reproductions of the artist's works, so if you're in the centre you might as well have a browse. The Walter Spies Festival is held every February — contact the Tourist Information Centre, Jl. Surapati, Denpasar, ph 223 602.

STSI (Academy of Dance)

The Sekolah Tinggi Seni Indonesia, formerly ASTI, is the Academy of Dance, located in the grounds of the Art Centre on Jl. Nusa Indah. A tertiary-level institution, it offers courses from undergraduate to masters level.

Visitors are welcome to observe dance and musical rehearsals at their leisure, or attend the regular dance and dramatic performances on the open-air Ardha Chandra stage. But the best time to visit is around June-July during the four-week Bali Arts Festival. A comprehensive program of gamelan and dance performances, as well as art and craft exhibitions, make this an event not to be missed.

Kokar

The Konservatori Karawitan, on Jl. Ratna, is a conservatory of music and dance. Whereas STSI is tertiary level, the conservatory is high-school level. The school was opened in 1962 and visitors are welcome to view the morning performances.

Kesiman

Take a drive through the old village of Kesiman and observe some fine examples of Badung architecture. The temple, Pura Kesiman, has a fine split gate in the old-Badung style, as opposed to the new Gianyar-style, reinforced concrete. The old palace, Puri Kesiman, is now a private residence and it's worth taking a peek.

SANUR

Sanur Beach, with its shimmering white sands and crystal-clear waters is idyllic, so it's little wonder that a cosmopolitan and luxurious village resort has blossomed. Surrounded by beautiful, lush tropical gardens, Sanur has managed to retain its serene beauty. Affluent tourists stroll leisurely along the beach in designer fashions; or swan about at the various soirees offered by the hotels. Although many young people stay in Sanur, typically the tourists tend to be older and richer — those who find Kuta a bit hectic.

It's ironic that Sanur is a tourist resort as many of its residents include Brahman and high-status families. And, as with all things Balinese, the highly religious atmosphere is juxtaposed with whispers of black magic.

Sanur was Bali's first international resort, and the Natour Grand Bali Beach Hotel (formerly the Bali Beach Hotel) was built in 1966 with reparations from the Japanese. President Sukarno hailed it as a symbol of modern Indonesia, but the Bali Beach Hotel is more like a monument to monstrosity. It eventually spawned a statute preventing the erection of buildings taller than palm trees.

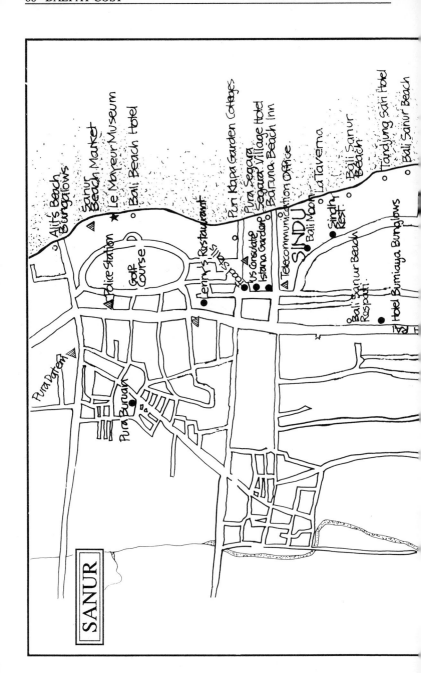

SANUR

Alit's Beach Bungalows
Sanur Beach Market
Le Mayeur Museum
Bali Beach Hotel
Puri Kapa Garden Cottages
Pura Segara
Segara Village Hotel
Baruna Beach Inn
Telecommunication Office
SINDU
Bali Moon
La Taverna
Sindhu Rest.
Bali Sanur Beach
Tandjung Sari Hotel
Bali Sanur Beach
US Consulate
Istana Gardena
Lenny's Restaurant
Police Station
Golf Course
Bali Sanur Beach Respati
Hotel Bumiaya Bungalows
Pura Dgren
Pura Buruan

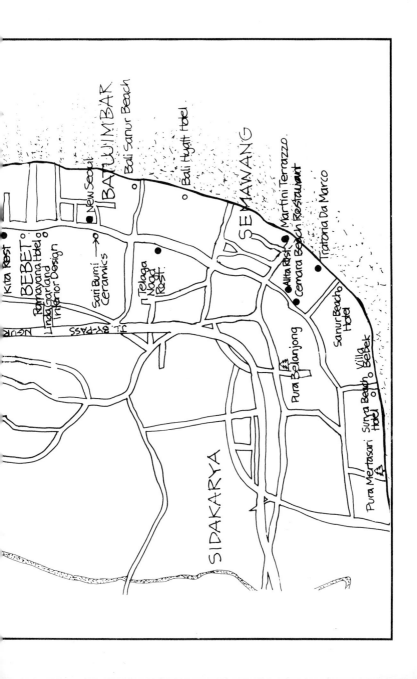

HOW TO GET THERE

By Taxi

From the airport take a taxi. Fares are fixed (Rp12,000), and tickets can be purchased from the taxi desk outside customs.

By Public Bemo

There are two bemo stops in Sanur, one north of the village opposite the Natour Grand Bali Beach Hotel, the other south on the main street near the By-pass road. Bemos do not run from Sanur to Kuta, so you must change in Denpasar.

By Hiring a Bemo

Bemos can be chartered from anywhere on the island to any destination, for a price. What that price will be, is largely determined by inexplicable factors. Shop around and bargain.

By Car

Sanur is 7km (4 miles) from Denpasar; 8km (5 miles) from Kuta; and 28km (17 miles) from Ubud.

TOURIST INFORMATION

Sanur has no tourist bureau, so either visit the tourist offices in Denpasar or make inquiries at your hotel.

ACCOMMODATION

Although Sanur is no longer *the* place to stay (Nusa Dua has usurped that title) there are still many first-class hotels. Prices for one night's accommodation should be used as a guide only, and are in US$. The telephone code is 0361.

5 star Hotels

These hotels are on the beach and include facilities such as bars, restaurants, shops, swimming pool, air conditioning, hot water, a fridge and complete room service. All major credit cards are accepted and prices are subject to the 15.5% tax and service charge.

Bali Hyatt, Jl. Hyatt, ph 288 271. Built on 15 ha (36 acres) it boasts five restaurants, four bars, a mini-golf course, tennis court, sauna, gymnasium, disco, and 15 shops. One of the pools even has a replica of Goa Gajah. Rooms from $160; suites from $290.

Natour Grand Bali Beach Hotel, Jl. Brigjen Ngurah Rai, ph 288 511. Bali's first big hotel, it was substantially remodelled following a fire in 1992. At the northern end of Sanur Beach, it has 600 rooms in a ten-storey tower. With a nine-hole golf course, ten-pin bowling alley, football field, children's playground, theatres, seven restaurants, six bars, a supper club, a cafe, local banks, shops, galleries and airline offices — it has just about everything. Rooms $120-$130; suites from $280.

4 star Hotels

La Taverna, Jl. Danau Tamblingan, ph 288 387. Old-world charm with all the modern-day comforts. One of the nicest beach-front hotels with semi-detached bungalows or family units. Rooms $90-$130; family $160; suites $195.

Sanur Beach Hotel, Semawang, ph 288 011. Four restaurants, two swimming pools, playground, tennis court, badminton, windsurfing, snorkelling, and a comprehensive fitness centre. Rooms $130-$180; suites from $300.

Tandjung Sari Hotel, Jl. Danau Tamblingan 41, ph 288 441. This hotel is one of Sanur's oldest and most elegant hotels and many jetsetters stop here. An intimate hideaway right in the middle of Sanur. Rooms $230-$290.

Segara Village Hotel, Jl. Segara Ayu, ph 288 407. Beachfront two-storey cottages. Caters for children. Rooms $65-$130; suites $235.

Surya Beach Hotel, Jl. Mertasari, ph 288 833. At the southern end of the beach so it's very quiet and has all first-class amenities. Rooms $95-$165.

Villa Bebek, Cnr Jl. Pengembak and Jl. Mertasari, ph 32 507. Three self-contained villas with personal staff.

Orchid Villa, Jl. Hyatt, ph 288 334. Has three fully self-contained bungalows. Room $90.

3 star Hotels

Most 3 star hotels are a walk from the beach, but otherwise they usually have the same amenities as the 4 star hotels. Of course there's a 15.5% tax and service charge.

Alit's Beach Bungalows, ph 288 576. Close to shops and restaurants. Room $40-$50.

Baruna Beach Inn, Jl. Sindhu, ph 288 546. Pretty bungalows with courtyard and water views. Breakfast, tax and service charges are included. Room $40-$50.

Bali Sanur Beach Bungalows, *Jl. Raya Sanaur*, ph 288 421.
There are three different locations: Respati, Besakih and Peneeda bungalows. All very close to the sea, Peneeda on the beach is the nicest. Room $45-$70.

Bumi Ayu Bungalows, Jl. Bumi Ayu, ph 587 517. Ten minutes' walk to the beach. Rooms from $50.

Janur Garden Hotel, Jl. By-pass Ngurah Rai, ph 288 155. As it's on the highway, few tourists stay. Room $40-$45.

Puri Kelapa Garden Cottages, Jl. Segara, ph 288 999. Set away from the beach the cottages are built around gardens and a pool. Room $50-$60.

Santrian Bali Beach Bungalows, Jl. Danau Tamblingan 10, ph 288 181. Private cottages on beachfront. Room $60-$75.

Sindhu Beach Hotel, Jl. Dano Tondano, ph 288 351. Beachside bungalows. Rooms $30-$80.

LOCAL TRANSPORT

By Public Bemo

There are numerous public bemos that wend their way around Sanur, from dawn to dusk. From anywhere to anywhere in Sanur costs about Rp200.

By Hiring a Bemo

Prices differ depending on the season, the tourist, and the mood of the driver. In the low season, US$5 should get you to Denpasar.

By Car

Renting a car is probably the best way to see Bali, and ditto for Sanur. **Here are a few rental agents:**
Avis, Bali Hyatt Hotel, Jl. Bali Hyatt, ph 288 271.
Bali Car Rental, Jl. By-pass Ngurah Rai, ph 288 539.
Holidays Company, Jl. Sanur Beach, ph 288 328.
Samudra Car Rental, Jl Sanur Beach, ph 288 471.

EATING OUT

There are numerous restaurants from which to choose. The restaurants in the **Bali Hyatt, Natour Grand Bali Beach and Sanur Beach Hotels** are all quite good but serve mainly **European food.**

The **Tandjung Sari Hotel** is renowned for its **rijstaffel,** a Dutch buffet of assorted goodies, and on Saturday nights there's a *legong* performance.

Or the **Sari Karya Bar and Restaurant offers Italian, Chinese, Indonesian and International cuisine** with different dance shows and live music (Jl. Bali Hyatt, ph 288 376).

Here is a list of restaurants you might care to try:

Balinese

Kul Kul, Jl. Bali Hyatt, ph 288 038. Specialises in Balinese ceremonial dishes.

Sanur Beach Market, Jl. Segara. Not just an array of tables on the beach, the spartan furnishings belie the richness of the food. The market is actually organised by a collective and the profits are used for the community. Dances are held on Wednesday and Saturday nights.

Chinese

Lenny's, Jl. Bali Beach, ph 288 572. The first Chinese restaurant in Sanur, it has a good selection of Cantonese as well as Indonesian food.

Telaga Naga (across from its proprietor, the Bali Hyatt). Indulge in Szechuan food in a relaxed atmosphere by the lotus pond.

Italian

La Taverna, just off Jl. Tandjung Sari, in the La Taverna Hotel. Eat good food by the sea, and be tempted by their pizzas straight from the brick oven.

Trattoria Da Marco. In south Sanur, Semawang. Purports to be the best Italian fare in Bali.

Japanese

Kita, Jl. Tandjung Sari, ph 288 158. For a nice change from pasta you can try sukiyaki, tempura, yakitori and others.

Korean

New Seoul, Jl. Danau Tamblingan.

Warungs

There are many *warung* which offer good, spicy, cheap food, especially in south Sanur on Jl. Bali Hyatt.

ENTERTAINMENT

Dance Performances

Many of the hotels have dance performances as do the restaurants. But you may want to see something different so here goes:

Wayang kulit or shadow puppet play is at the Mars Hotel every Tuesday, Thursday and Sunday from 6pm-9pm.

Frog dance at the Penjor Restaurant on a Sunday night at 7pm, ph 288 226. The *joged* is every Wednesday night, the *janger* every Friday night, and the *topeng* on Saturday night.

The *kecak* or monkey dance, which is not to be missed, is held at Tandjung Bungkak, on the way to Denpasar, every night from 6.30pm.

Nightlife

Subec Club is frequented by the locals, and thankfully, airconditioned.

Matahari in the Hyatt is where most of the tourists go to let down their hair, but be warned drinks are expensive; or try *No 1* on Jl. Tandjung Sari. *Rumours* is newly-opened and gaining favour.

SHOPPING

Like all the tourist centres in Bali, Sanur is filled with shops. In Kuta there's a better selection of shops and the prices are generally cheaper, however, Sanur tends to have more ceramic and antique shops which rival the best on the island.

Antiques

There are quite a few antique shops on Jl. By-pass Ngurah Rai, but beware of the genuine reproductions!

Sekar Tanjung, Jl. By-pass Ngurah Rai. A very curious little shop providing a potpourri of weird and wonderful things.

Tjek Lai, on the By-pass. Another good antique shop.

Books

Sanur Bookstore, Jl. Hyatt. Sells novels in English, international periodicals as well as books on Indonesia, all substantially cheaper than the bookshops in the big hotels.
Bali High Books, Jl. Semawang.

Pottery

Keramik Jenggala at Batu Jimbar has some interesting and original works.
Sari Bumi, Jl. Hyatt. Brent Hesselyn, a New Zealander, has been creating ceramic goods for Bali's hotels and restaurants for many years. Very difficult to leave without parting with some of your money.

Supermarket

Gelael Supermarket, Jl. By-pass Ngurah Rai. For all those little necessities, as well as wine, crackers and camembert.

Textiles

Many of the chain stores you see around Kuta and Ubud are also in Sanur, especially in the big hotels.
Nogo, Jl. Tandjung Sari. Designer wear using traditional *ikat* and *endek* fabrics. Purchase from the rack or have clothes made to order; and watch women relentlessly weaving.

Linda Garland

Linda Garland has won international acclaim as an interior designer. Her showroom, on Jl. Hyatt, has a wide selection of home furnishings. Fashionable but expensive.

SIGHTSEEING

Prasasti Belanjong

At Belanjong village, in the temple past the Sanur Hotel, is an inscribed stone pillar shaded by a lotus. It is Bali's earliest dated artefact. Only partially deciphered, the inscriptions suggest that it was erected in 914AD, by Sri Kesari Varma, a Javanese king. Reference is made to a military invasion against eastern Indonesia.

Coral Pyramid

At the end of Jl. Segara, is a small temple with a coral pyramid that supposedly dates back to pre-Hindu times.

Le Meyeur Museum

The former home of the Belgian painter, Le Meyeur, who resided in Bali from 1932. His wife, Ni Polok, has maintained the house as a museum since Le Meyeur gave it to the Indonesian Government in 1958. The house is quite impressive (notice the ornamental window shutters displaying carved scenes of the *Ramayana*) and his paintings hang inside.

Located behind the Natour Grand Bali Beach Hotel.
Open Sunday, Tuesday to Thursday from 8am-2pm;
Friday 8am-11am;
Saturday 8am-12.30pm;
Closed on Monday. **Admission Rp500.**

WATERSPORTS

If you'd like to do more than take a dip, say for instance, waterski, jetski, dive, parasail, windsurf or simply snorkel, try the big hotels. For diving try the Bali Marine Sports Dive Centre, Jl. By-pass Ngurah Rai, ph 287 872; or Oceana Dive Centre, Jl. By-pass Ngurah Rai, ph 288 652.

SERANGAN ISLAND

Turtle Island, as Serangan Island is sometimes known, is, of course, famed for its turtles. About a kilometre off the coast of Sanur, it has an area of 73 ha (180 acres). Some residents are engaged in farming corn, maize, peanuts and beans while others ply the tourist trade, but the island is principally concerned with breeding turtles.

Turtle meat is a ceremonial delicacy and is often eaten as *sate* or finely ground for the dish *lawar*. The green turtle, which lays its eggs on the shore, is easily caught by villagers who simply wait for the turtles to hatch their eggs and then turn them on their backs. The eggs are also a delicacy and turtle shell is sold for jewellery and ornaments. Unfortunately, the turtle is a lucrative catch, and the green turtle, especially, is rapidly approaching extinction. In fact, most countries' Customs Officers will confiscate any turtle products, so don't bother buying any.

Serangan Island also has a special temple, Pura Sakenan. Situated on the north coast of the island, the temple dates back to the 10th century. The complex, in fact, houses two *pura*: the first has only a single obelisk (the throne of Dewi Sri, the goddess of agriculture); while the second, the larger *pura*, is typically Balinese.

How To Get There

The *jukung* fishing boats that line Sanur Beach will ferry tourists to Serangan Island and return, for Rp20,000. Motorised *prahu* can be hired for Rp40,000 an hour to sail around the lagoon.

The trip from swampy Suwung, directly opposite the island, is much cheaper (Rp3000) and quicker. But, Suwung is about 6km (4 miles) from Sanur, just off Jl. By-pass Ngurah Rai (the turn-off is well sign-posted), so a car is recommended.

To Nusa Lembongan and Nusa Penida

Across from Sanur are the outlines of two islands that actually shadow Serangan Island. *Prahu* can be hired from Sanur to Nusa Lembongan, the smaller of the two islands, and the fare will depend on the number of people travelling, as well as the cost of the petrol the amount of which will vary with the tide, the current and the wind.

For more information see the section on Klungkung, which is the regency to which these islands belong.

KUTA AND LEGIAN

Kuta, so it's said, was a sleepy fishing village, and a hideaway for criminals, reprobates and exiles. While cynics might say that little has changed, they're wrong. Kuta has fine restaurants, great surf, cocktails with profane names, and profound sunsets. It's a shopper's paradise, a drinker's fantasy, and a claustrophobic's nightmare. Dogs howl in competition with the local *gamelan* orchestra, and crowing roosters remind ragers it's time for bed. Short sun-filled days melt into hot nights of oblivion. Kuta's not for everyone, but that's not a bad thing.

Kuta's history is less than illustrious. It was the port for the Majapahit Empire, and Gaja Mada, a Minister of the Empire, possibly built a fortress at Kuta — "Kuta" means fort.

In the 19th century, Mads Lange, a daring Dane, fled Lombok and settled in Kuta, establishing a trading post, and later built a coconut oil factory. Lange managed to ingratiate himself with the Raja of Badung, as well as the Dewa Agung, and was pivotal in the negotiations between the Balinese rajas and the Dutch in the tumultuous 1846-1850 period. From this time, Kuta was a port o' call for ships to resupply and repair.

In 1936, Robert and Louise Koke, two Californians, came to Bali and were captivated by its beauty. Their legacy? The Kuta Beach Hotel, the first tourist joint. It wasn't until the 1960s that tourists began to take stopovers in Bali, and Kuta beach was *the* place to stay. Long-haired hippies, enamoured of the place, found families willing to let rooms and *losmen* were born. Opportunists, aware of the value of a dollar, established rest-aurants and shops, and Kuta grew into a spirited, even crazy village. Ever since, tourists have sought the sultry sunsets, sand, surf, shopping and sex — not necessarily in that order.

In the early 1970s, Legian was still a separate village, a place of respite for those indifferent to Kuta's offerings. Now the two villages are virtually one. Kuta and Legian are totally self-contained, and there is no need to venture beyond their limits. But, there is much, much more to Bali than Kuta.

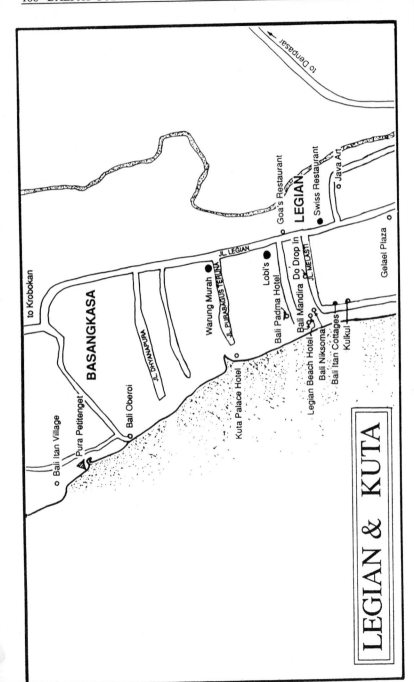

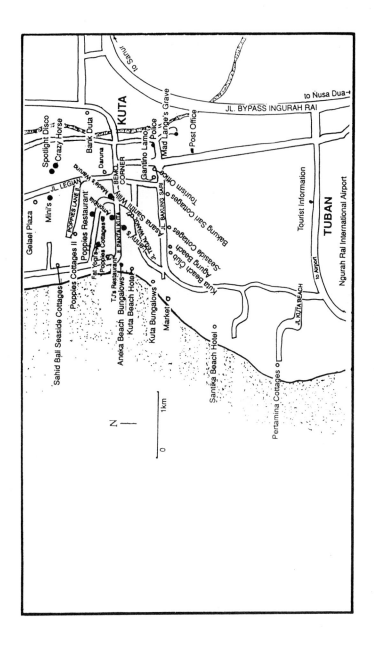

Swimmers Beware!
The goddess of the sea is said to claim a victim each year, but most tourists explain drownings due to the sometimes perilous undertow and strong currents. Always swim between the flags and stay near the crowd.

HOW TO GET THERE
Most travel agents organise transfers from the airport with accommodation. But those without prior reservations will have no problem finding transport.

By Public Bemo

From the airport, provided you're not over-burdened with luggage, take a public bemo from Jl. Airport Ngurah Rai, just outside of the gates (Rp500).

By Hiring a Bemo

Probably not the nicest introduction to Bali are the mobs of bemo drivers that beseech tourists to hire their bemos. The fare is negotiable and that's where the problem lies. Bemo drivers are a breed unto their own and make used-car salesmen look honest. Unlicensed Bemos are not permitted into the airport compound, but this does not prevent these persistent people from annoying tourists. Take a taxi.

By Taxi

The easiest form of transport from the airport is by taxi and fares are fixed. Simply purchase a ticket from the taxi desk in the arrival section of the airport. Taxis generally charge Rp800 flagfall and Rp800 per kilometre. The fare to south Kuta is Rp4500, Rp6500 to north Kuta and Rp12,000 to Seminyak.

TOURIST INFORMATION
There is a Government Tourist Information Office Jl Benesari

(near the corner of Jl. Legan), Kuta, ph 753 540. The staff are extremely helpful and will provide a map and a leaflet with events for the month.

ACCOMMODATION

Hotels in Kuta and Legian run the gamut of accommodation, from 5 star hotels to very cheap losmen. Around December and July it is imperative that rooms are booked in advance. Prices for one night's accommodation are in US$, and should be used as a guide only. The telephone code is 0361.

5 star Hotels

All the luxury hotels have full amenities and offer various restaurants, pools, sporting facilities and 24 hour room service. Prices are subject to a 15.5% government tax and service charge, and there are high season supplements.

Bali Oberoi, Jl. Kayu Ayu, Petitenget, ph 751 061. 75 rooms. This is *the* place to stay in Bali — grand but discreet. Coral rock bungalows are scattered throughout landscaped gardens and facilities include restaurants, bars, tennis court, swimming pools, water sports, bank, shops, beauty salon and outdoor theatre. And, of course, the hotel has its own secluded beach. It has everything. Room $175-$240; villas from $400.

Bali Padma, Jl. Padma 1, Legian, ph 752 111. Recently opened, it is just as good as the Oberoi, but not as well known. Room $120-$155; suites $195-$295 - or the Presidential suite for a mere $1760.

Pertamina Cottages, Jl. Kuta Beach, Kuta, ph 751 161. Originally an executive haven, Pertamina offer spacious Western-style rooms with old-world charm. The cottages are set amidst 11 ha of landscaped gardens. Very close to the airport. Room $125-$180; suites from $480.

4 star Hotels

All hotels have a restaurant and bar, swimming pool, and rooms have hot water and airconditioning. Prices are subject to a 15.5% government tax and service charge.

Bali Intan Cottages, Jl. Melasti 1, Legian, 751 770. A short walk to the beach. Rooms $80-$95; suites from $175.

Bali Mandira, Jl. Padma, Legian, ph 751 381. Located on the beach. Room $85-$105; suite $180.

Intan Beach Cottages, Jl. Bakung Sari, Kuta, ph 751 507. Great location, across from the beach and on the cusp of Kuta and Legian. Rooms from $80.

Kul-Kul, Jl. Pantai Kuta, Kuta, ph 752 921. A walk to the beach. Room $85-$115; suites from $350.

Kuta Beach Hotel, Jl. Pantai Kuta, ph 751 361. Great location on the beach. Rooms from $90.

Kuta Palace Hotel, Jl. Pura Bagus Teruna, Legian, ph 751 433. Room $95-$120.

Legian Beach Hotel, Jl. Melasti, Kuta, ph 751 711. Room $60-$250. Located on the beach.

Sahid Bali Seaside Cottages, Jl. Pantai Kuta, ph 753 855. Room $80-$100.

Santika Beach Hotel, Jl Kartika, Tuban, ph 751 267. Beachfront hotel caters for the family. Has tennis court. Room $60-$170.

3 star Hotels

These hotels usually offer very good facilities but without sporting attractions. Most rooms have airconditioning and hot water, and breakfast is often included. Rates include the 15.5% tax and service charge.

Agung Beach Bungalows, Jl. Bakung Sari, Kuta, ph 751 263. Room $30, breakfast and tax included.

Aneka Beach Bungalows, Jl. Pantai Kuta, ph 752 892. Across the road from the beach. Room $40-$65; suite $140-$210.

Asana Santhi Willy, Jl. Tegalwangi 18, Kuta, ph 751 281. Great location and surprisingly quiet. Room $20-$35.

Bakungsari Cottages, Jl. Bakung Sari, Kuta, ph 751 868. Near the action but surprisingly quiet. Room $30-$40.

Bali Niksoma Beach Cottages, Jl. Padma, Legian, ph 751 946. On the beach. Northern end of Legian and right on the beach. Room $25-$80.

Bali Summer Hotel, Jl. Pantai Kuta 38, Kuta, ph 751 503. Room $30-$40.

Garden View Cottages, Jl. Padma Utara 4, Legian, ph 751 559. In a quiet back lane a few minutes' walk from the beach. Room $40.

Kuta Beach Club, Jl. Bakung Sari, Kuta, ph 751 261. A ten-minute walk to the beach. Room $45.

Kuta Bungalows, Jl. Legian Kelod (Gang Benesari), Kuta. A walk from the beach. Room $40.

Palm Beach Cottages, Jl. Pantai Banjar Segara, Kuta, ph 751 661. Short walk to the beach. Room $50-$55.

Poppies Cottages, Poppies Gang, Kuta, ph 751 059. A short walk to the beach. Self-catering facilities available. Exceptional for the price, but best to book. Room $60.

Ramayana Seaside Cottages, Jl. Bakung Sari, Kuta, ph 751 865. About 200 metres from the beach. Room $40.

Sandi Phala, Jl. Kartika Plaza, Kuta, ph 751 865. Overlooks the beach. Room $40.

Budget Accommodation

There's an abundance of *losmen* in Kuta and Legian with rooms for as little as US$5 a night. Prices are often negotiable, depending on the duration of stay. Location is of the utmost importance — Kuta can be very noisy — as is cleanliness. **The best idea is to shop around.**

LOCAL TRANSPORT

Really, the best way to get around Kuta and Legian is to walk — how else could you manage to stop at all those shops!? But you may need transport to some of the outlying attractions.

By Public Bemo

Kuta's transport hub is **Bemo Corner,** on the crossroads of Jl. Pantai Kuta and Jl. Legian. From Bemo Corner there is a regular service to Jl. Padma, Legian. The public bemos have particular routes, but will stop anywhere along the route to pick up. See **Local Transport** in the section on Denpasar.

To travel to any major villages from Kuta, first go to Denpasar.

To Denpasar, public bemos pick-up at bemo corner and unload at the main market or Tengal terminal (see **Local Transport** entry in the **Denpasar** section).

To Sanur, catch a bemo to Tengal terminal, change for Kereneng terminal then change there for Sanur.

To Ubud, first go to Tengal, then change for Batubulan, and from there its Ubud.

By Hiring a Bemo

Along Jl. Legian are a species of predatory bemo drivers that incite momentary mirth, followed by frustration, then irritation. The prices are negotiable, but shop around and ask other travellers. Group charters can be cheap, but if you're travelling alone the prices can be exorbitant.

By Taxi

Taxis are often located at, or can be contacted through, the larger hotels.

By Car

The best way to see Bali is to hire a car. Unfortunately, navigating the one-way streets in Kuta can be torturous and finding a park, miraculous. The closest petrol station is on Jl. Kuta Raya.

For information on car rental agencies see the "Local Transport" entry in the "Travel Information" section.

EATING OUT

Kuta has a multitude of restaurants and warung, catering for a multitude of nationalities. Savour international cuisine or scoff a burger. Cappuccinos, jaffles, sandwiches, chocolate cake, milk shakes, burgers, steak, baked dinners, vegemite, KFC, McDonalds, ice cream parlours — Kuta has them all.

The tourist favourites are Poppie's, TJ's and Made's Warung. Poppie's is one of the oldest restaurants in Kuta, the food is consistently good, and the surroundings lush and leafy. Make a reservation.

TJ's has great Mexican food, a good cocktail bar and pleasant atmosphere.

Made's Warung, which has everything from baked dinners, to cheesecake to padang food, is the place to be seen, and being open-fronted makes for good people-watching. Excellent food complemented by a cosmopolitan atmosphere.

Here are a few names and addresses:

Bakery

Cafe Francais, Jl. Kartika Plaza. Great place for brekky.
Sri Dewi Bakery, Jl. Legian.
Twice Pub, Jl. Legian Kuta (Poppie's Gang No. 2).
Za's, Jl. Legian. Known for its breakfast menu but also serves pastas, curries, etc.

Chinese

Golden Snack Chinese and Seafood Restaurant, Jl. Bakung Sari (inside the Pasar Seni).

German

Mama's German Restaurant, Jl. Legian. Surprisingly authentic food.

Indian

Griya Delta, behind Panin Bank, just off Jl. Legian. One of the few Indian restaurants on the island, and highly recommended. Possesses the only tandoor in Bali.

Indonesian

Gantino Lamo, Jl. Bakung Sari. A wondrous assortment of padang dishes will be delivered to your table before you can say "bagus makan" (good eating).

Made's Warung, Jl. Pantai Kuta. A nasi campur to titillate the taste buds.

Depot Viva, Jl. Legian. Basic but good food.

International

Made's Warung, Jl. Pantai Kuta. From padang to cappuccino, and a lot in between. Try the diabolically decadent chocolate cake.

Poppie's, Poppie's Gang 1.

Italian

Fat Yogi's, Poppie's Gang.

Il Pirata, Jl. Legian. Busy pizzeria and open very, very late.

Pesona, Jl. Legian.

Japanese

Yashi, Pertamina Cottages, Jl. Kuta Beach. The best Japanese food in Bali.

Daruma, Jl. Legian (near Bemo corner). Boasts the full complement of Japanese seafood dishes.

Sushi Bar, Jl. Legian. Expensive but good sushi and sushimi.

Mexican

TJ's, Poppies Gang. Enchiladas, tacos, tostadas — all taste sensations!

Seafood

Bali Indah, Jl. Buni Sari, Kuta.

Lenny's, Jl. Pantai Kuta, Kuta, ph 751 833.

Bali Seafood, Jl. Kartika Plaza (opposite Bintang Hotel). Choose your dinner from the tank and know that it's fresh!

Swiss

Swiss Restaurant, Jl. Legian, on the right just before Jl. Melasti (near the Swiss Consulate). Bratwurst and fondue to name a few.

Fast Food

Pizza Hut and KFC can be found on Jl. Raya Kuta. There is also a KFC and Swensen's Ice Cream Parlour in the Gelael Plaza, Jl. Legian 10 and Burger King is just opposite. There's also a McDonalds and another KFC further along Jl. Legian.

WHERE THE ACTION IS...

Kuta

If Kuta is busy by day, it's just warming up. Once sated on Kuta's culinary delights it's off to the bars for light refreshments and respite, before assaulting the discos.

The night clubs aren't lively till late, so try **Casablanca's** for a cocktail or two; have a game of pool in the **Peanuts complex** (Jl. Legian); or if you're into people-watching, have a coffee at **Made's Warung.**

For those into *pub crawls,* you've come to the right place — **Peanuts Disco** (ph 751 920) and **Bali-Aussie** (ph 751 910) will arrange transport. **The Sari Club** (SC) is always overflowing with Australian visitors, as are most places.

When the clock strikes midnight, if you haven't changed into a pumpkin, put on your dancin' shoes. At the Peanuts complex, there's a couple of discos, **Peanuts, Spotlight** and **Koala Blu,** which cater to the Top 40 crowd. **Crazy Horse** in the same complex has live bands and a gargantuan video screen. Enjoy it while you can because the complex is soon to be developed into a shopping centre.

North of Peanuts alley is a newly-opened and busy **Hard Rock Cafe**.

Bruna, on the Kuta Beach road, is especially animated on a Sunday night. **The Bounty,** on Jl. Legian, has a large video screen and films are shown nightly (yes, it's actually a replica, of sorts, of the Bounty).

Legian

In Legian, two beach front discos (haunts for the slightly more chic) are **66** (**Double-Six**) (second lane to the north of Jl. Padma, off Jl. Legian), and **Chez Gado-Gado**. 66 has a restaurant with good Italian and seafood. Chez Gado-Gado (might as well be in the Sahara, but any bemo can get you there), is more sophisticated in a yuppie-hippy-ish way.

ENTERTAINMENT

Kuta

Kuta is not the place to be enthralled by traditional dances, Ubud owns that distinction. But if you don't intend to leave Kuta, Claytons performances are held at the local *banjar*, the village meeting place.

The *legong* dance is performed at the new Banjar Tegal Kuta, behind Jl. Buni Sari every Tuesday and Saturday night at 8pm. The *kecak* is held at Banjar Buni Kuta on a Sunday night, and excerpts from the *Ramayana* are performed every Thursday and Monday nights. In Legian, at Banjar Pekandelan, on Jl. Legian Tengah, watch out for the flag which heralds a dance performance. The *banjar* usually charge about Rp5000 a performance.

A performance you may hear without even leaving your hotel is the tones of the local *gamelan* orchestra practising in the banjar. Another free, but not so welcome, act is that of howling dogs or *anjing* — those despicable pariahs that are the antithesis of everything Balinese.

SHOPPING

Kuta and Legian are a bargain-shopper's paradise: from small boutiques selling "designer" goods, adjacent to dusty little shops displaying dusty little items, to pedlars offering beachwear.

For paintings and carvings, go to Ubud.

Antiques

Beware of genuine reproductions. Whether an item is cheap or expensive, it may well be a fake. There are a number of shops along Jl. Pelasa. Be astute.

Polo, Jl. Legian, south of Jl. Melasti.

Books

Kerta I Bookshop, Jl. Pantai Kuta.

Cassette Tapes

There are copious cassette shops throughout Kuta and Legian. The quality has improved and most shops have quite good selections. Since Indonesia signed a copyright agreement, cassettes shops are supposely 100% legal. Cassettes sell for around Rp8,000 and CDs are more expensive at around Rp26,000.

Mahogany Music (Jl. Legian) has the biggest range and the staff really know their music. Generally, there is not much difference in prices at various stores but some give a discount if you purchase ten cassettes.

Clothes

In the last couple of years Kuta has developed a reputation for its rag trade. Many young designers from all around the world have come to Bali to establish their own businesses. Years ago, cheap mass-produced beachwear was ubiquitous. Now, there's still plenty of cheap clothing, but there are also some very chic boutiques with designer fashions. Most of the good clothes shops have fixed prices and by Kuta standards they're expensive — but by international prices they're a bargain. All relative isn't it?! Most take credit cards, although the vendor will charge about 6% which is the rate the banks charge.

Baik Baik. A young Balinese designer with a flare for the dramatic, works with traditional and modern fabrics styles.
Galang Dua Koleski, Jl Pantai Kuta (not far from Bemo Corner). Has a treasury of fine antique-style clothes, with lots of lace and intricate embroidery.
Hey, Jl. Pantai Kuta. Sells casual clothing for men and women.
Indigo, Jl. Legian. A chain store specialising in batik shirts for men and women. The styles are definitely more "up-market" than those sold in the markets.
Kekal, Jl. Legian and also at Jl. Pantai Kuta. Sedate designer clothing for women.
Kuta Kidz, Bemo Corner. Illustrates the Balinese philosophy of dressing children in miniature adult fashions. Very cute!
Mr Bali, Jl. Legian. One of the original menswear shops and now, one of a chain.

Curios
Borneo Art Shop, Jl. Legian.
Kaliuda Art Shop, Jl. Legian.
Kuta Art Market, Jl Bakung Sari, near the beach.

Jewellery
For the filigree silver for which Bali is so famous, Celuk is the best place. But Kuta has the best range of fashion and costume-style jewellery. Most of the designer shops have fixed prices but are competitive, and the designs are original.

> Any purchases you make from the child-hawkers roaming the streets are plated inferior metals.

Leather Goods
Kuta is the best place to purchase leather goods. If you want clothing, most shops will make the garments to measure. See

the "Shopping" entry in the "Travel Information" section.
Gecko, Jl. Legian.
Mr Kuta, Jl. Legian.
Romada, Jl. Bakung Sari.

Photography

If you have any camera problems go to Prima Photo on Jl. Thamrin in Denpasar. But if you simply want to develop your film, there are a number of one-hour processors along Jl. Legian.

SIGHTSEEING

Tour companies, as well as hotels, offer a variety of tours around the island. Prices differ as to sights, number of people travelling, and the state of the transport. The guides usually speak fluent English and are enamoured of their island — their enthusiasm is often contagious.

Besakih

This tour takes about eight hours and visits Batubulan, Celuk (famed for its silver), Mas (woodcarving), Gianyar, Klungkung, Kerta Gosa, Goa Lawah (Bat Cave) and Bali's state place of worship, the "mother temple", Pura Besakih. The temple is actually a huge complex of temples and shrines on the foothills of Gunung Agung. If you're not planning to venture that way yourself, this tour is a must!

Kintamani

A day tour which travels north to Gunung Batur, an active volcano, and the third highest mountain in Bali. From Kintamani, the view of Batur and its lake is spectacular — not a bad way to spend a day.

Tanah Lot

This is usually an afternoon tour to witness the splendour of the majestic orb as it descends below the horizon. Seeing the celebrated Balinese sunsets is magical in itself, but at Tanah Lot the sunset throws the temple into sharp relief — enchanting! (see the entry in the chapter on Tabanan.)

Ubud
This tour usually takes half a day, and visits Celuk, Batuan, Mas, Bedulu, and Ubud. Again, if you're not planning to travel to these places, at least take a day tour.

OUTLYING ATTRACTIONS

Pura Petitenget
Along the beach, north of the Bali Oberoi, is the temple of Petitenget. Built entirely of white coral, the temple was founded by the famed priest, Nirartha, and shares a common forecourt with the *subak* or irrigation co-operative's temple, Pura Ulan Tanjun.

Ulu Watu
If you have your own transport take a trip to Ulu Watu and see one of Bali's most beautiful pieces of architecture. See the section below on "Ulu Watu" for more information.

BUKIT PENINSULA

"Bukit", literally hill, properly denotes the area south of Nusa Dua; nevertheless, the entire peninsula, from the narrow isthmus of Jimbaran, is limestone. Thousands of years ago the huge barren plateau was probably separated from the mainland, but it is now connected by a narrow isthmus. Made of limestone, the Bukit is not conducive to agricultural pursuits, and its rugged white cliffs and austere plains provide a striking contrast to the verdant inland.

JIMBARAN

On the western side of the Bukit Peninsula, past the airport (along the old airport road), is Jimbaran. An old fishing village, Jimbaran has a quaint restaurant/hotel with panoramic views of the bay. A small temple, Pura Ulun Siwi, has an ornate split gate and a multi-tiered *meru* tower. A little past the village market, and off to the right, is a group of *kepuh* trees which mark the site of a cemetery used for the temporary internment of bodies before cremation. A sign indicates the Hotel Puri Bali, then it's a few more hundred metres to Jimbaran Bay.

The main road that meanders to Nusa Dua, by-passes Jimbaran Bay, which is definitely a good thing. White, sandy beaches and **very few people make this a nice quiet retreat.** The bay is protected by a reef, and the surf doesn't break so much as lap. On this island of contrasts, beauty has its counterpoint: on the eastern side of the peninsula is Suwung, an uninviting swamp.

The temple on the beach is Pura Muaya, but continue the ascent to an impressive view of the airport and bay. The road stops at the **government youth hostel centre**, so backtrack to the old road, and continue to the next right, which rambles to Salakan. Visit Pura Sarin Buana and the huge basin-like formation, Gua Peteng, along the way.

From Salakan to the old main road, continue south and the next left is the Universitas Udayana, about 2km (1 mile) from the highway. Back to the main road again, and continue south to Simpangan, then to Bongol village and the forked intersection. The left reaches to the east and eventually, Nusa Dua. The right path leads to Ulu Watu.

Take the right, and the next right leads to the fishing village of **Cengiling.** While many male villagers fish, the women are particularly adept at, and are famous for, weaving *subak* sashes. Beyond this point, its a pleasant walk to the cave temple of Pura Balangan — take a torch. Backtrack again to the main road, heading towards Ulu Watu. The road climbs Gunung Ingas, the highest point on the peninsula at 203m (666ft). The next village is Pecatu, and the road west leads to Ulu Watu.

ULU WATU

The temple at Ulu Watu forms one of the most magnificent views on the island. During the day, with a brilliant azure sky and waves crashing beneath, the temple is impressive. But as the sun slowly descends, the temple acquires a mystical quality, the limestone masonry assuming a golden appearance.

The sheer cliffs of Ulu Watu are believed to be the petrified ship of Dewi Danu, goddess of the waters. The temple, Pura Luhar Ulu Watu or "temple above the stone", is perched precariously on a precipice of 90m (295ft). Originally designed by a Javanese priest, Empu Kutaran, in the 11th century, it was a sanctuary for the Mengwi Dynasty up to 1891. The temple is one of the six most important temples on Bali and is part of the Sad-Kahyangan group. The priest, Nirartha, is said to have visited the temple in order to achieve unity with the godhead or *moska*, and you'd be a real stoic if you weren't moved by its beauty and atmosphere.

The temple is carved from Bukit limestone and has three compounds.

The **outer courtyard** has a split gate with garuda wings, while the second courtyard has a monstrous image of Siwa flanked by two elephant-looking Ganeshas.

The sacred **inner courtyard** has a *meru* shrine. Of course, all this beauty must have an antithesis, and indeed it does.

Beware of a very brazen band of monkeys who delight in pilfering visitors' belongings in attempts to procure food.

Surfing

Ulu Watu is also **a surfing wonderland of sorts,** and is known to have an almost perfect surfing break all year round. It is also said to be *one of the best left-handers in the world.* Best ask the guys at The Surf Shop, on Jl. Legian in Kuta, or at Amphibia nearby. The next break down from Ulu (as it is known by surfers) is Padang-Padang. Because of its proximity to a cliff, it is challenging — dangerous is probably a better word.

How to get there

Unfortunately, the only public bemos to Ulu Watu depart from Tegal terminal in Denpasar and don't travel via Kuta.

Those without a car will have to charter a bemo, which can be quite expensive, about Rp40,000 (US$21) for a round trip. Generally, the locals are not happy about driving on the narrow, pot-holed roads, but the area is worth seeing.

From Kuta follow the old airport road, past the airport, continuing south for miles (see the section on Jimbaran). From the carpark it's a 300m walk to the temple.

Suluban Beach

For the surfers, just before the Ulu Watu carpark is a sign to *Suluban Beach*, **the** surf beach. Young boys will gladly provide transport by motor bike, for a price, of course. You cross fields for about 2km to a small parking area, and again young boys can be hired to carry boards and gear for the 40-minute walk to the gorge, or motorbikes can traverse the area with great difficulty. There are quite a few *warung* which cater to famished surfers. To reach Padang-Padang, a track continues from Saluban or there's access for bikes.

NUSA DUA

Nusa Dua is far, far from the madding crowd. Although the name means "two islands", Nusa Dua is in fact two small raised headlands connected to the mainland by sand tracts. Once upon a time, the small village called Bualu was a coconut plantation. But the Indonesian government, concerned with the unchecked sprawl of Kuta, had a cunning plan. The idea was to create a prestigious international resort, while minimising the impact on local life. Funded by loans from the World Bank, the government successfully transformed a desolate, isolated area into a burgeoning luxury hotel complex. First came the Baulu Hotel, the forerunner to the School of Tourism, followed by bigger and better hotels.

Nusa Dua is a carefully-crafted paradise. If Kuta is developing out of control, Nusa Dua is growing to plan. True, there are no losmen nor street vendors nor riffraff, and life is immeasurably discreet, but the sterile serenity and battalion of security guards lining the major thoroughfares are hardly comforting. Such is life!

HOW TO GET THERE

By Taxi

From Ngurah Rai airport, taxi fares can be purchased at the taxi desk for about US$7. Alternatively, the hotels will arrange transport from the airport for the same price as a taxi fare.

ACCOMMODATION

All hotels are 5 star, and prices in US$ are for one night's accommodation and should be used as a guide only. Rates do not include the 15.5% tax and service charge.
The telephone code is 0361.
Nusa Dua Beach Hotel, PO Box 1028, Denpasar, ph 71 210. The first hotel in Nusa Dua, it welcomes guests with a huge split

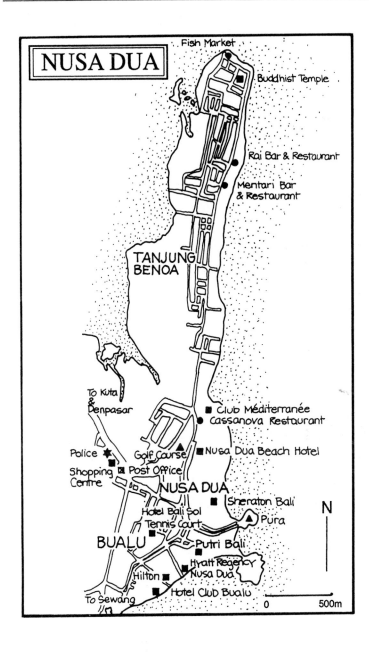

NUSA DUA

Fish Market

Buddhist Temple

Rai Bar & Restaurant

Mentari Bar
& Restaurant

TANJUNG
BENOA

To Kuta
&
Denpasar

Club Méditerranée
Cassanova Restaurant

Police

Golf Course

Nusa Dua Beach Hotel

Shopping
Centre

Post Office

NUSA DUA

Sheraton Bali

Hotel Bali Sol

Pura

Tennis Court

BUALU

Putri Bali

Hyatt Regency
Nusa Dua

Hilton

Hotel Club Bualu

To Sewang

N

0   500m

gate or *candi bentar*. This is where the then-president, Ronald Reagan stayed — need I say more? Rooms from $140; suites from $350; with private pool $1200.

Hilton Bali, ph 71 102. 540 rooms. Designed to harmonise with the environment, the hotel includes a children's play centre and complete watersport facilities. Rooms $130-$200; suites from $450.

Club Mediterranee Nusa Dua, PO Box 7, Denpasar, ph 71 521. 350 rooms. Supposedly a fun place to visit, but you must first join the club. Contact your local travel agent and assess the package deals on offer.

Melia *Bali Sol*, PO Box 1048, Tuban, ph 71 510. 500 rooms. Frequented by Japanese tourists, it's owned by the Spanish Sol chain and reflects more of Spain than Bali. Room $105-670.

Hotel Village Bualu, PO Box 6, Denpasar, ph 71 310. Probably the cheapest hotel in Nusa Dua, a couple of minutes walk to the beach. And it's the only hotel in Indonesia that has a PADI (Professional Association of Diving Instructors) teacher. Room $80; suite $115.

Putri Bali, PO Box 1, Denpasar, ph 71 020. An old-style luxury hotel with cosy cottages as well as rooms. Room $150-$170; suites from $300.

LOCAL TRANSPORT

Taxi

Taxis are available from all hotels.

Car Rental

Avis Rent-A-Car is located in the Nusa Dua Beach Hotel, ph 71 210.

EATING OUT

Nusa Dua has over 30 international restaurants from which to choose. All the hotels offer theme nights and dance performances on a regular basis.

Outside of the hotel complex, a number of independent restaurants are beginning to emerge. Not within walking distance of the hotels, most restaurants offer free transportation — just give them a call.

SHOPPING

A number of clothes boutiques are located out of the hotel complex, as are the typical stock of souvenir shops. Really, nothing compares to Kuta and Legian for shopping.

Galleria complex, ph 71 662. A large airconditioned shopping mall. If it weren't for the colourful masked characters wandering around, you'd never believe you were in Bali.

Supermarket

Tragia Supermarket. The supermarket offers an hourly shuttlebus service to all hotels. For all the mundane essentials — pate de foie gras, brie, caviar...

BENOA

North of Nusa Dua, the village of Tanjung Benoa was formerly the port for Denpasar. Now it's a mooring for visiting yachts and has the potential to become a luxury resort. Although a small village, a Bugis mosque and a Chinese Klenteng temple bear testimony to the variety of peoples who have made Benoa their home.

Benoa has a few medium-priced hotels and two very good restaurants. The *Rai Seafood Restaurant* has a cocktail bar and superb seafood, and right next door is the *Mentari Ming Garden*, whose bar is also amply stocked, and the food comparable. They both look out to Serangan Island which makes a great backdrop.

Why not cruise around Bali or its various satelites on a luxury yacht. **Trade Wind Yacht Charter** (PT Tourdevco) offers numerous organised tours or devise your own itinerary (PO Box 1081, Tuban, Denpasar, ph 231 591).

NOTES

GIANYAR

Gianyar lies in the heart of Bali. Separated from the regency of Badung by the Ayung river, the regency of Gianyar extends south to the coastline, north to the mountains a few kilometres below Gunung Batur, and shares its eastern border with Bangli. Gianyar is also said to be the *cultural* heart of Bali and has the status of a sanctuary for those who wish to escape from the south. Although the town of Gianyar is the regency's capital, most travellers make a beeline for Ubud.

The second most populated regency after Badung, Gianyar derives most of its income from tourism.

From Denpasar to Ubud, a chain of villages specialising in various arts and crafts seduces rupiah-laden visitors.
Batubulan is known for its stone carvings;
Celuk for its silver; *Sukawati* for its shadow puppets;
Batuan for its paintings; and
Mas for its woodcarvings.

But Gianyar isn't simply known for its cultural attractions. The Pejeng-Bedulu region, which lies between the locally revered rivers, the Pakerisan and the Petanu, bears testimony to Gianyar's ancient past. A brass drum, known as the "Moon of Pejeng", is one of the oldest antiquities on the island and is probably more than 2000 years old. The hermitage of Goa Gajah at Bedulu, dates back to the 10th century, as do the holy springs at Tirta Empul. In any historical summary of things Balinese, fact is blurred with fiction: the people prefer to believe that the "Moon of Pejeng" was a natural satellite that fell to earth; and that the giant, Kebo Iwa, carved the architectural stone masterpieces with his thumb nail.

History

Historians believe that Gianyar was established in the late 18th century, when Dewa Manggis, after much intrigue, was installed as the first Raja of Gianyar. Previously the territory had been divided among the kingdoms of Klungkung, Badung, Bangli and Mengwi. The neighbouring rajas were infuriated by their loss of land, and the following decades witnessed constant battles between the states.

A couple of generations later, the Dewa Manggis VII visited the Dewa Agung (Raja of Klungkung) to sue for peace. Not about to let bygones be bygones, the Dewa Agung imprisoned the Raja of Gianyar and reclaimed the land. But Badung and Tabanan successfully conspired to reclaim the reclaimed land, and divided it between themselves. The Dewa Manggis' two sons escaped incarceration and after a prolonged battle, they re-established the kingdom of Gianyar.

The new Raja of Gianyar requested that the regency be received as a Dutch protectorate, and in 1900 the Dutch agreed. While the rest of southern Bali suffered from Dutch invasions and power-broking between themselves, Gianyar prospered.

ON THE ROAD TO UBUD

BATUBULAN

A bridge over the Biaung River marks the border separating the regency of Badung from the regency of Gianyar. The first village after the border is Batubulan (the name means "moon stone"), and it is famed throughout Bali for its guardian statues carved from soft volcanic stone. Visitors are more than welcome to visit shops and may observe the artists at work. Originally, stone works were found only in temples and palaces, but now the art can be seen everywhere. Fantastic figures are posted at intersections, and bas-reliefs with Western themes are carved on facades of buildings. Many images are inspired by the Hindu epics of the *Ramayana* and *Mahabharata*. Some well-known carvers are Made Leceg, Wayan Mergog and Made Sura who have shops on the main road - they'll organise shipment back home of purchases.

Batubulan is also the home of the *barong* dance. Every morning, from 9am to 10am the barong is performed by four different groups at four temples along the main road.

CELUK

The village of Batubulan ends at the intersection marking the turn-off to Celuk. Renowned for its intricate, filigree silver, Celuk is definitely the best place to buy silver. The silversmiths will create any designs requested, or pieces can be chosen from the displays. **There are a plethora of silver shops along the main road,** and visitors can observe the artists at work, instructing their apprentices.

Celuk is the best place to buy silver provided that you're not accompanied by a guide who will receive a percentage of the purchase - obviously raising the final price.

SUKAWATI

Sukawati is located midway between Denpasar and Ubud, and was once the residence of the 18th century raja, Dalem Sukawati. **The village is best known for its puppetmasters, the *dalang,*** who not only make the puppets, but also write the plays and perform them. Many of the puppetmasters travel around the island performing with their troupes; or they can be commissioned to write plays or make a special set of puppets.

Few people realise that Sukawati has a colony of artisans who create wind chimes - take a walk down the main road and you will hear them.

Sukawati also has a complex of temples that is second only to that at Besakih. There are six temples representing the *sad kayangan* group, all of which are dedicated to the prosperity of Bali and the Balinese.

The *pasar seni* or art market, is the place from which craft-shop owners buy their goods, and the prices are generally cheaper than anywhere else on the island.

BATUAN

For centuries, Batuan has been a hive of artistic activity, thanks to the prevalence of *Brahman* families, and their support of the arts. Dancers, musicians, carvers, painters, and even foreign artists work in Batuan, and travellers are free to browse through the studios.

Batuan dancers are known for the *topeng* (mask) dance, as well as the exquisite, court dance called the *gambuh*. Two *gambuh* troupes are the only groups which still perform the ancient dance, and visitors can see the performances daily.

Batuan is probably best known for its painters. There are two styles of painting associated with Batuan. Under the tutelage of Spies and Bonnet, artists adopted a "realistic" rather than "stylised" attitude to the human form. The paintings are intricately drawn and details are shaded by a technique called *sigar mangsi*, literally "ink fragments", using sombre reds, browns and blacks. The second style of painting was developed by Dewa Ketut Baru, who worked with black ink on a white background. The Puri Lukisan Museum at Ubud has an excellent exhibition of paintings in the Batuan styles. Wooden panels, screens, statues and *topeng* masks, all carved by Batuan artists, are the best buys in Bali. The Kesenian Art Gallery, on the road to Mas, also sells Batuan's wooden handicrafts. Next door is the Jati Art shop which has a good display of traditional paintings for sale.

MAS

Although Mas means "gold", the village is a centre for woodcarving. Traditionally, woodcarvers were Brahman priests who sculpted scenes from the *Ramayana* and *Mahabharata* epics, to adorn temples. Later, during the 1930s, under the influence of Walter Spies and others, a more realistic style developed and, since the 1970s, Mas has blossomed into a woodcarving, dare I say, Mecca.

Typical *Mas* carving is highly polished, and made of superior wood. Walk into any studio and watch young apprentices chiselling gnarled pieces of wood into elegant figurines. The village of Mas is supposedly where the priest Nirartha built a hermitage, and the temple, Pura Taman Pule, is built on the site of Nirartha's former residence.

TEGES

The village of Teges is divided into two communities: to the east, is Teges Kanginan, famous for its dancers and musicians; and to the west, is Teges Kawan, whose villagers are woodcarvers. The sculptors of Teges Kawan are lauded for their interesting fruit arrangements - you may have noticed one or two in Kuta.

PELIATAN

Although Teges and Peliatan are distinct artistic communities, they are really the same village. Peliatan is best known for its graceful *legong* dance, and a group of Peliatan dancers was the first to perform Balinese dances abroad. Today, a number of accomplished dance groups perform the *legong* for visitors. The village is very much at the forefront of dance, and classical and modern styles develop concurrently. A modern dance troupe performs the *barong nandini* "ballet", which combines modern choreography with traditional theatrical techniques.

Peliatan has more than 15 *gamelan* groups, and has the only women's *gamelan* in Bali. The Smar Pegulingan Gong orchestra has travelled the world, and performs in Peliatan weekly (ask at the tourist office in Ubud).

Don't miss the exceptional gallery of former painter Agung Rai, at the southern end of Peliatan. The different bungalows that contain the gallery have been designed and built to reflect the style of paintings they house. There's a permanent exhibition of Balinese paintings, as well as works for sale.

Peliatan is a 20-minute walk from Ubud or a short bemo ride (Rp100).

PENGOSEKAN

Until recently, Pengosekan was almost isolated from the surrounding villages, enabling its painters to develop a unique character to their work. A poor village of artists, they painted together and decided to purchase supplies communally, and in 1979, the group formed a co-operative, calling themselves the Pengosekan Community of Artists. **Famous for their paintings of whimsical animals,** the community's works were exhibited overseas, and for some time the group experienced relative prosperity. The co-operative, as such, no longer exists, but there are a few in the community who still continue to create works in the inimitable Pengosekan style. Others participate in the mass-production of painted tissue boxes, fruits and frames, which are exported overseas.

To get there, walk down the Monkey Forest Road from Ubud Raya, following the road as it swerves to the left past the forest. Turn right to Pengosekan (which is signposted) or left to Peliatan.

UBUD

Hidden amid green forests and protected by lush valleys lies Ubud. Often touted as the cultural heart of Bali, many people flee the south in search of the **real Bali** and some never venture past Ubud. Despite the increase in tourism in the last ten years, Ubud remains a peaceful village where traditions are preserved.

History

Ubud dates back to the 8th century, when a Hindu priest, Rsi Markandeya, and his disciples discovered the intersection of two rivers - a good phenomenon for Hindus - and built a temple at the site. The temple is called Pura Gunung Lebah; and the village, Campuhan, means the "meeting of two rivers". Further up the mountains, Ubud became the home of his disciples.

In the late 18th century, the Raja of Gianyar requested that

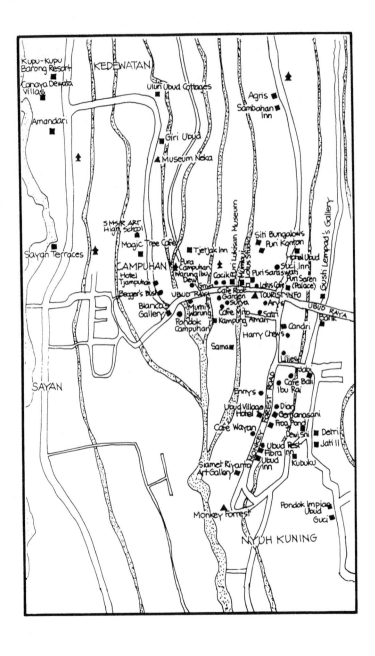

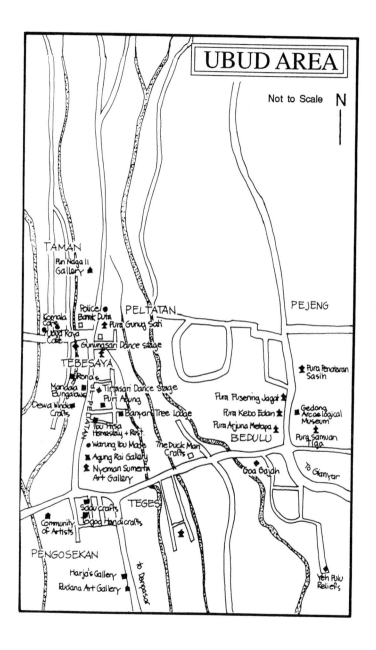

UBUD AREA

Not to Scale N

TAMAN
Pun Naga II
Gallery

Police
Komala Batik Duta
Cafe
Ubud Raya Pura Gunug Sari
Cafe
Gunungsari Dance Stage
TEBESAYA
Rona's
Mandala
Bungalows Tirtasari Dance Stage
Dewa Windu Puri Agung
Crafts
Ibu Prisa Banyan Tree Lodge
Homestay + Rest.
Warung Ibu Made
Agung Rai Gallery The Duck Man
Nyoman Sumerta Crafts
Art Gallery

PELIATAN

PEJENG

Pura Penataran
Sasih

Pura Pusering Jagat
Pura Kebo Edan Gedong
Pura Arjuna Metapa Archaeological
Museum
BEDULU Pura Samuan
Tiga

Goa Gajah to Gianyar

TEGES
Sadu Crafts
Community Tegoa Handicrafts
of Artists

PENGOSEKAN

Harja's Gallery to Denpasar
Rudana Art Gallery

Yeh Pulu
Reliefs

the kingdom be protected by the Dutch. While the rest of Bali suffered under the harsh policies of the Dutch, Gianyar prospered. Cokorda Sukawati, a local prince, befriended young artists and enticed them to live in the village. The young sculptor Lempad, an enemy of the Raja of Bedulu, accepted the prince's offer, and assisted in the creation of the Puri Saren palace and the adjacent temple. The German artist, Walter Spies, accepted an invitation to make Ubud his home, and settled in Campuhan on the site of what is now the Hotel Tjampuhan. Miguel Covarrubias was enchanted by pictures of Bali, and Rudolph Bonnet heard about the island on the grapevine. Both artists made Bali their home.

In 1936, Spies and Bonnet founded the Pita Maha society for artists, under the auspices of Cokorda Sukawati. Although the group disbanded at the outbreak of war, an artistic collective-consciousness had evolved which was to augment and direct the village's cultural heritage. In 1953, Cokorda Sukawati and Bonnet founded the Puri Lukisan Museum - a monument to the fine arts in Bali.

During the 1950s, Arie Smit, a Dutch painter, founded the Naive School of Painters in Penestanan. The group was dedicated to drawing and painting subjects ignoring conventional dictates. Han Snel, another Dutchman, ingratiated himself with the locals, and still lives in Ubud, as does Antonio Blanco.

Ubud is not only a concentration of Balinese talents, it is also a happy marriage between East and West. No doubt Bali will change as tourism increases but the Balinese resilience and willingness to utilise foreign influences will hopefully enable the continuation of a rich cultural heritage.

HOW TO GET THERE

By Public Bemo

In Denpasar, bemos depart from Kerengeng terminal for Ubud and cost Rp1000.

By Taxi

A taxi from the airport costs around Rp18000 and Rp35000 with airconditioning.

By Car

Ubud is 25km (16 miles) from Denpasar and takes about forty-five minutes by car. From Kuta, the distance is about 34km (21 miles).

TOURIST INFORMATION

The Bina Wisata Tourist Office, on Ubud Raya, near the main crossroad, will supply information about festivals and dance performances, as well as tours to Kintamani and Candi Dasa. They are also rental agents for cars, motorbikes and bicycles.

ACCOMMODATION

The range of accommodation in Ubud has expanded considerably and there are too many hotels to mention them all. Shop around.

Prices are in $US for one night's accommodation, and do not include tax and service charges, but should be used as a guide only. Telephone code is 0361.

5 star Hotels

All 5 star Hotels have airconditioning, and usually include transfers.

Hotel Tjampuhan, Campuhan, Ubud, ph 975 368. Extravagantly furnished bungalow-style rooms located amongst waterfalls and tropical gardens, and there's even a natural spring pool. Room $40-$80.

Kupu Kupu Barong Resort, Kedewatan, Ubud, ph 975 478. High above the Sayan Valley, these bungalows are ideal for families. The restaurant is excellent. Bungalow $305-$635.

Ulun Ubud Cottages, Sanggingan, Ubud, ph 975 024. Overlooking Campuhan River, on the outskirts of Ubud, ner the turn-off past the Neka Gallery. There's a steep descent to the restaurant that would not suit children or the elderly. Room $60-$70.

4 star Hotels

Rates are all inclusive.
Cahaya Dewata Country Villas, Kedewatan, Ubud, ph 975 495. Relatively large hotel with full amenities. Room $55-$80.
Siti Bungalows, Jl. Kajeng, ph 975 699. Owned by painting personality, Hans Snel, the charming bungalows are in the centre of Ubud, but tucked away in a side-street behind the Lotus Cafe. Rooms from $40-$50.
Ubud Village Hotel, Monkey Forest Road, ph 975 069. In the middle of Ubud, overlooking rice terraces. Intimate rooms with private courtyard. Swimming pool has sunken bar. Room $40.

3 star Hotels

Dewi Sri Bungalows, Jl. Hanuman, Padang Tegal, Ubud. Quiet location with pool and restaurant. Room $25-$50.
Fibra Inn, Monkey Forest Road, ph 975 451. Small gardens with swimming pool. Room $30.
Kori Agung Bungalows, Penestanan, Ubud. Room $25.
Pondok Impian Ubud, Jl. Raya Pengosekan, ph 95 253. A fifteen minutes' walk from the centre of Ubud. Room $35.

Budget

Losmen are everywhere in Ubud. Rooms are available for as little as $4 - they're spartan but clean, and families are welcome. Try along Monkey Forest Road or Jl. Hanuman.

LOCAL TRANSPORT

Ubud is easily explored on foot. The main road is Ubud Raya, and the heart of Ubud is the junction where the Monkey Forest Road meets Ubud Raya (in front of the Puri Saren palace). To the west is the Peliatan T-intersection; to the east, is Campuhan and the suspension bridge.

By Public Bemo

Public bemos depart from the "terminal" in front of the market (to the east of the palace), from dawn to dusk. Bemos travel to surrounding villages for about Rp300 and to Denpasar for Rp500 (though tourist fares are gaining favour).

Renting Transport

The Bina Wisata Tourist Office has a rental service that is highly recommended.

Motorbikes (100cc) cost about Rp10,000 per day, and bicycles can be rented for about Rp3000. Suzuki Jimneys can be rented for about Rp30,000 daily, and cheaper for a month..

EATING OUT

Ubud doesn't have fast food outlets - thank the gods! -but it does have many and varied restaurants.

Monkey Forest Road

Lilies. Everything from Steak Dianne to satay to fish. And fabulous cakes!

Enny's Restaurant. More like a *warung* in style and prices, but has a good selection of Indonesian delights.

Harry Chew's. Off the Monkey Forest Road, in the street next to the field. A popular *warung* that specialises in Chinese and Javanese food.

Cafe Wayan. Excellent Indonesian and European food. Above average prices but worth it.

Main Road - Ubud Raya

Ubud Raya. Reasonably priced, Japanese and Indonesian food.

Nomads. Past the markets towards Peliatan. Open until late, it has a good cocktail bar and surprisingly good seafood.

Night Markets. This is the best place to eat if you want to try the real thing - very cheap and never disappointing. Here I sampled my first Indonesian desert, *ice campur* - a concoction of pink, white and green things, that is highly recommended - ask, and the ladies will make it with boiled water.

Mutiara. A simple *warung* with a multitude of food.

Ary's. Near the tourist office. Another reasonably priced *warung*.

Han Snel, Kajeng Lane. Intimate and romantic atmosphere. The service is very good, but it's expensive by Indonesian standards. The mini-rijstaffel is a local legend.

Cafe Lotus. Ubud Raya, in front of the lotus pond. For cosmopolitan people, or those that like to watch them. The view of the pond with lotus in bloom as well as the ambience, makes this a nice place to spend some time. Pate, pasta, veal, Moet (and lots more) - for all those delights you thought you'd never find in this part of the world.

Mumbul's Garden Terrace Cafe, Ubud Raya. Overlooks a pretty gully. Homesick for a sandwich? Go no further!

Murni's Warung. On the main road near the suspension bridge. Murni's also caters for travellers with homesick tummies.

Pondok Campuhan. Across the suspension bridge. Attractive decor and food to match.

Beggar's Bush. **The pub in Ubud.**

Sayan and Kedewatan

Ayung, Cahaya Dewata Country Villas, Kedewatan. Stunning views - a great place for an afternoon drink.

Kupu Kupu Barong Resort Restaurant. Acclaimed locally, savour the superb food and the view.

ENTERTAINMENT

The Bina Wisata Tourist Office has information on dance performances in Ubud and the surrounding villages. Most performances cost Rp5000 or higher where transportation is included. Ticket-sellers often roam the streets selling tickets to performances at the palace.

Sunday

Kecak at Bona 7pm, or at Padang Tegal at 7pm. Padang Tegal is much closer, and both performances are very good. Also enquire at the Bina Wisata for the Peliatan *gamelan* performance at 7pm.

Monday

Kecak at Bona, 7pm. *Legong* at Puri Saren palace, 7.30pm.

Tuesday

Raja Pala at the Banjar on Monkey Forest Road, 8pm. Dramatic excerpts from the *Mahabharata* in Banjar Teges, Peliatan, 7pm.

Wednesday

Wayang kulit (shadow-puppets) at Oka Kartini's, Ubud Raya, at 8pm. *Kecak* at Bona, 7pm. *Ramayana* at Ubud Kelod, 7.30pm.

Thursday

Gabor dance from the *Mahabharata* at Ubud Kelod, 7.30pm. *Topeng* (mask dance) at Pura Pengosekan, 7.30pm. *Legong* at Pura Dalem, Peliatan, 7.30pm. *Bimanya* Dance at Panca Arta, Ubud, 8pm.

Friday

Barong at Puri Saren, Ubud, 6.30pm. *Kecak* at Bona, 7pm. *Legong* at Peliatan at 6.30pm. *Calon arang* dance at Menara Restaurant (near the tourist office), 8pm.

Saturday
Legong at Puri Saren, Ubud, 7.30pm.

SHOPPING

Antiques
Pondok Seni in Pengosekan has interesting items, some bordering on garish. *Murni's Collection* (Kunang Kunang) has an array of antiques, also clothes, silver, pottery and cloth.

Books
Ubud Bookstore, opposite the lotus pond, has a good range of books on Indonesia and Bali. *Ubud Newsstand* on Ubud Raya sells newspapers. *Neka Museum* also has a range of books.

Clothes
In the last couple of years, Ubud has improved in the fashion stakes. The days of sombre, dowdy batik tent dresses are numbered! Try **Lotus Studio**, near the coffee shop, for designer wear. Quite expensive, but they are originals. **Murni's Collection,** down from the warung, has some interesting clothes.

Silver
There's a surplus of silver shops in Ubud to rival Celuk. Although fixed-prices are the order of the day, prices are competitive, and often-times bargaining is permissible. Shop around for prices and styles.

Markets
In the centre of town, in a two-storey cement eyesore are the markets. Clothes, baskets, carvings, and food galore.

Paintings

Ubud is the best place to purchase paintings. Browse through the various galleries (listed below) for the styles and prices and then venture into the artists' homes - they're only too happy to show their displays to "rich" tourists. The other thing about paintings is, you might think you have an original, and while it won't be a print, there may be several others, exactly the same, hanging in various shops and restaurants. **The moral - look before you buy!**

MISCELLANEOUS

There are a number of **one-hour photo development store**s on Ubud Raya.

For the **main chemist (*apotik*), Police Station and Telephone Exchange** head east towards Denpasar, and turn left at the Peliatan T-intersection.

Bank Duta is also at the T-intersection, and BCA Bank is not far from Nomads on Ubud Raya. If you simply need to change money there are various money changers, who have very competitive rates.

The **Post Office** is on Ubud Raya, east towards the Peliatan T-intersection, and post restante services are available.
(Open from 8am to 2pm Monday to Saturday). More conveniently, there are a number of postal agents along Ubud Raya and Monkey Forest Road who are just as reliable.

MUSEUMS AND GALLERIES

Puri Lukisan Museum

The Puri Lukisan or "Palace of Paintings" was opened in 1953 by Cokorda Gede Agung Sukawati and Rudolf Bonnet both of whom helped establish the esteemed Pita Maha art society in the 1930s. The society's aim was to encourage painting and the museum marked the deliberate separation of painting from religious life.

The museum has three buildings set amidst landscaped gardens and a pond. Two buildings have permanent and slightly dusty exhibitions, and emphasis is on an historical perspective of Balinese painters. The curator is very enthusiastic and helpful. Unfortunately, the exhibitions are becoming dilapidated - victims of the climate and general neglect. The building in the centre houses an exhibition of paintings by a co-operative and the works are for sale. Note the painters you like and visit them in their village.

Open from 8am - 4pm; admission Rp500.

Neka Museum

About a kilometre past the Campuhan suspension bridge is the best art gallery on the island. The museum has a superbly presented treasury of paintings collected by Wayan Suteja Neka, who has organised the extensive collection according to styles. Incidentally, Fine Arts students at Udayana University must be familiar with the works in the Neka Museum in order to graduate. Works include those of indigenous painters as well as Bonnet, Spies, Smit, Meier, Covarrubias and Friend.

Neka Gallery

Former home of Neka, Bali's foremost art dealer, located on Ubud Raya, east, towards Peliatan.

Munut Gallery

An exhibition of contemporary Indonesian and Balinese artists. Open from 9am - 5pm.

Lempad Gallery

The former home of the revered painter, I Gusti Nyoman Lempad, fellow member of the Pita Maha group. Renowned for his risque pen and ink drawings, the gallery is worth a peek for the insights into pre-tourist Ubud.

Agung Rai Gallery

On the main road in Peliatan, it houses an excellent collection of paintings.

Antonio Blanco's Gallery

Past the suspension bridge on the left. Blanco's gallery has an exhibition of some of the Philippine artist's works, featuring erotic and fantasy drawings of his wife, who runs the gallery. The collection is illuminating for its view on the Bali of yesteryear.

SIGHTSEEING

Puri Saren

In the heart of Ubud is the palace of the Cokorda Agung family. It was rebuilt in 1917 after an earthquake, and features doors carved by Lempad. Next door, is the royal family's temple, Pura Pamerajaan Sari Cokorda Agung.

Puri Saraswati

Behind the lotus pond and the former palace, Puri Saraswati, (now a hotel) is the Pura Saraswati, "temple of learning". Walk north to Ubud's navel temple, Pura Puseh.

The Monkey Forest Temple

At the bottom of Monkey Forest Road is the Monkey Forest, and yes, it's the residence of a very bold band of monkeys. Admission is Rp500 and a scarf must be worn around the waist. Walking past the ticket gate turn left before the forked path and up a slight incline to the Pura Dalem or "temple for the dead". The left-hand path leads around to Monkey Forest Road and the right-hand path leads to the main temple.

PEJENG - THE HOLY ROCK ROUTE

Pejeng, designated as the area between the Pakerisan or "Kris River" and the Petanu or "cursed River", includes the majority of Bali's antiquities. One could easily spend an entire day, travelling around this rather small area, taking in the sights.

GOA GAJAH

In Bedulu, about 2km (1 mile) from the T-intersection at Ubud, is the Elephant Cave or Goa Gajah. According to myth, Dalem Bedulu, the King of Bedulu, was a devout Buddhist given to decapitating himself before meditating. One day, the courtiers who were instructed to mind the King's head, lost it, and quickly replaced it with that of a pig. The king, understandably ashamed of his appearance, concealed himself in a tower and forbade visitors to view the grotesque sight. News of the king's condition reached Java, and the prime minister of the Majapahit Empire, Gajah Mada, was ordered to meet the king of Bedulu and verify the tale. Of course, Gajah Mada found the pig-headed king, so to speak, and caused the king's ruination. The cave at Goa Gajah, was the real head of the King of Bedulu, which eventually fell back to earth. Another myth is that Bedulu's minister, the giant Kebo Iwa, carved the rock-face with his thumbnail.

Goa Gajah, called the Elephant Cave because archaeologists thought it looked like the head of an elephant, was once a Buddhist monastery. Situated above the Petanu River, the complex of temples and baths is testament to the influence of Buddhism before the arrival of Hinduism. The entrance to the cave is over 2m (6ft) high and features the whimsical carving of a man with huge eyebrows and moustache - his mouth is the opening. Inside is a dimly lit T-shaped chamber, with niches carved in the wall (don't forget to take a torch). At each end of the "T" is a statue of Ganesha, Siwa's son. Of course, Ganesha is a Hindu god, but there are statues of Buddhist figurines in the pavilion adjacent to the cave, and down the fifty or so steps behind the compound are statues of Buddha. It's all a bit confusing, but the Buddhist Balinese established the compound first, and as Hindu influences filtered through, Hindu religious motifs were added.

Admission is Rp500 and visitors should be sartorially resplendent in sash and sarong (or long pants). As is the custom, temple gear is for hire.

YEH PULU

About a kilometre from Goa Gajah is a 14th century life-size frieze, depicting scenes of rural life. Unfortunately, few tourists visit the site as it entails a walk through rice fields, but it's easy to find and the walk isn't difficult. Between Goa Gajah and the Bedulu crossroads, follow the cobblestone road on the right (south), past *warung* to the rice fields. From there it is a walk to the site.

Carved into the side of a rock, the relief (25m x 2m - 82ft x 6.5ft) is either a series of isolated vignettes on daily life or a story. The carvings are very different from any others found either on Bali or Java; the scenes are naturalistic, and do not conform to the traditional styles found elsewhere.

Framed by a leave motif, the impressions include: hunters attacking a boar; a farmer hoeing a field; a woman furtively peeking behind a door; a woman pulling a horses tail; culminating in a relief of Ganesha, Siwa's elephant-headed son. Interestingly, towards the end of the frieze, smaller animal scenes seem to parody the human scenes, for instance, a frog stabs a snake and a monkey steers another monkey by pulling its tail. The carving was "discovered" in the 1920s by the Dutch artist, Nieuwenkamp, although the Balinese had known about it for years. According to legend, the carvings are the handiwork of the giant, Kebo Iwo, who is said to have etched them with his thumbnail.

THE MOON OF PEJENG

Enshrined in the temple of the moon, Pura Panataran Sasih, is the monumental drum, the "moon of Pejeng".
(North from Bedulu, the temple is on the right as you enter the village of Pejeng.)

Cast in a single piece, it is the **largest drum of its kind found anywhere in Asia.** It probably dates back to the bronze age, around 300BC, but no one knows for sure. And whether it was made on the island or was a gift from other lands is a total mystery. But, archaeologists have excavated at least one stone mould, so obviously drums were cast on Bali.

The drum, which looks more like a gong with a waist, is decorated with geometric patterns and stars, and four garish faces (thought to be the earliest-found representations of the human face). Fable has it that the drum was one of the earth's moons which dropped to the earth. Of course, there's always an embellishment - a thief found the moon and intimidated by its brightness, urinated on it, causing the moon to explode. One of the fragments dropped to the earth in the form of the drum. Other fables say that the drum was a wheel of the chariot of the moon, and another still, says it was the earring of the giant, Kebo Iwa.

The drum is truly enigmatic, and will remain so, for it is perched high in a shrine and very difficult to see - take binoculars. Admission is by donation and as the drum is in a temple, a sash is mandatory.

BEDULU

The village of Bedulu was once the abode of the Pejeng kingdom, the last bastion of Buddhism on the island, before the arrival of the Majapahit empire.

Pura Samuan Tiga, the temple east of the Bedulu crossroads, is notable because of its early Hindu statuary dating from the 11th century. The temple may have been built by the wandering priest Empu Kuturan.

The archaeological museum, **Gedong Arca,** is about 2km (1

mile) north of the Bedulu crossroads. One of only five such museums, it contains pre-Hindu artefacts such as neolithic stone axe heads and adzes, bronze jewellery, Chinese ceramics, as well as Hindu relics. One of the features is a huge stone sarcophagus, an antiquity from the days before cremation. The museum is open every morning until midday.

PURA KEBO EDAN

Travelling a few kilometres north of Bedulu, past the archaeological museum, is the "mad buffalo temple", Pura Kebo Edan (it's on the left). Inside the compound is a 4m (13ft) high statue, probably of Bima, one of the brothers from the Pandawa family in the epic poem *Mahabharata*. The awesome figure, complete with horns and fangs, has a huge (one hesitates at saying realistic) set of the male genitalia, with four pins pierced through it. (Apparently, this was a custom in South-east Asia to increase the woman's pleasure). Snakes are entwined about its feet and wrists, and it stomps on a dead body. Notice that the cadaver's eyes are open.

PURA PUSERING JAGAT

A 14th century temple, the Pura Pusering Jagat derives its name from "navel of the world", which is how the former residents thought of Pejeng. The temple houses some fine statues, the most notable being the "Pejeng Vessel" which is dated from 1329. The 75cm (29in) vessel depicts the "churning of the ocean", a story from the *Mahabharata*, which recounts the search for the elixir of life - quite apt given the vessel is still used for holy water.

GUNUNG KAWI

South of the village of **Tampaksiring** are the monumental royal tombs and hermitage of Gunung Kawi, the "Mountain of the Poet". Built in the 11th century, the tombs are thought to have been built by Anak Wangsa, the ruler of Bali, for himself and his concubines, as well as his brother King

Erlangga of Java. The tombs are hewn from the rock-face of the gorge of the sacred Pakerisan river.

Walk past the customary souvenir vendors and up a steep path of stairs for a view of the magnificent gorge. The blackened tombs set amidst the lichen-covered ravine and cool waterfalls make this an austere place. As one enters the site, the four concubines' tombs are on the left, and across the Pakerisan River are the five royal tombs and adjacent hermitage.

The tombs are carved niches or *candi* and have no interior compartments, they are merely sombre facades. Adjacent to the royal tombs is a monastery complex comprising several caves and a particularly deeply-hewn chamber with windows and a skylight. Further to the right and past rice paddies is the tenth tomb.

PURA PEDARMAN

South-east of Bedulu, in the village of Kutri, is the Pura Pedarman temple. Enshrined in the temple is a 2m (6.5ft) high statue of Durga, the goddess of death. The six-armed goddess was the wife of Siwa, although many believe that the statue was crafted after the evil Mahendratta (wife of Udayana and mother of Erlangga), known in myths as Rangda the witch.

TIRTA EMPUL

A couple of kilometres out of Tampaksiring lies the spring of Tirta Empul. Legend tells of a demon king named Maya Danawa who believed that he was the supreme ruler. Of course, Siwa, the supreme god, was maddened by the mortal's delusions of grandeur, and sent an army of heavenly warriors, commanded by Indra, to defeat the fraud. During the battle, the dastardly demon king murdered the warriors by poisoning their drinking water, Indra shot his magic arrow into the ground to tap the earth's "elixir of life" (*amerta*), and presto! the sacred Pakerisan gushed forth. Maya Danawa attempted to escape by changing into a rock in the stream, but the warriors found him and murdered him - his blood became the cursed Petanu River. So cursed, the Balinese refused to use the river, even for irrigation purposes, until the 1920s.

The supposed curative and cleansing powers of the spring of Tirta Empul make it one of the most revered sites on Bali. Behind the outer courtyard, and shaded by a magnificent banyan tree, are two pools, one for men, one for women. The spring flows from the inner sanctum of the temple which is protected by a wall lest it be defiled. The complex was restored in 1969 and is meticulously maintained.

Surrounded by these beautiful stone carvings and cleansing waters, one can't help noticing the huge concrete monstrosity on the hill. It was built by the late President Sukarno as a weekend retreat - he supposedly wanted to be near the sacred grounds.

GIANYAR TOWN

Gianyar town is the capital of Gianyar regency. Although devoid of the tourist rush, it is still an interesting place to visit.

The town is famed for its *babi guling* (roasted duck) and fine *endek* (Balinese cloth in which the weft (lengthwise) threads are dyed before the cloth is woven). Along the main road are various textile shops where women weave the cloth on huge wooden looms.

In the heart of the town of Gianyar is one of the few remaining traditional Balinese palaces. It is presently inhabited by Anak Agung Gede Agung, former Foreign Minister and heir to the throne of Gianyar. The *puri* was originally built in the 18th century, and in the 19th century, when the Dewa Manggis' sons escaped imprisonment by the Dewa Agung of Klungkung, they regained power and fled to the palace. The palace was rebuilt on the site of a priest's home and in fact "Gianyar" is an abbreviated form of "new priest's home". The sons sought Dutch protection from neighbouring rajas, and the empire flourished as a Dutch protectorate.

Next to the palace is the royal family's temple, the Pura Langon or "temple of beauty".

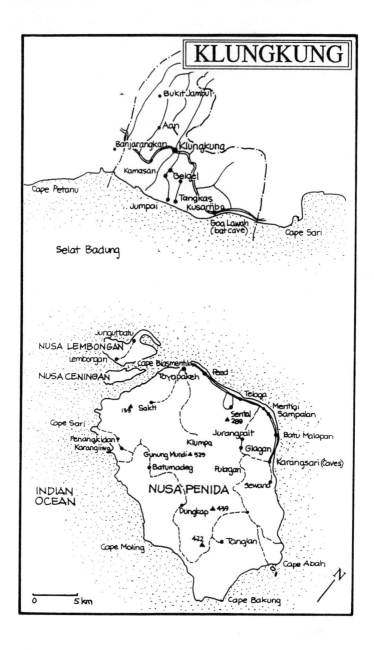

KLUNGKUNG

The tiny, prosperous regency of Klungkung is nestled between the regencies of Gianyar to the west, Bangli to the north and Karangasem to the east, and includes the islands of Nusa Penida and Nusa Lembongan. The smallest regency on the island, Klungkung is the abode of the illustrious Gelgel royal family.

History

Gaja Mada, the Javanese general, conquered Bali in 1343, and claimed the island as part of the Majapahit Empire, establishing a court at Samprangan, near modern Klungkung. As the empire buckled under the pressure from the Islamic Mataram Empire, the Majapahit entourage, led by the emperor's son, fled to Bali.

In 1515, the emperor's son established a court at Gelgel, near modern Klungkung, and bestowed upon himself the title of Dewa Agung, the "Lord of Lords". He empowered the noble *Brahmana* and *Satrya* to divide and administer the island, and slowly extended the Empire to East Java, Lombok and Sumbawa. And with power, wealth and prestige, the Gelgel Empire witnessed a cultural renaissance - Bali's "Golden Age".

Nothing lasts forever, and successive generations watched the power and wealth dwindle. In 1868, an ambitious general, Maruti, conquered the Raja of Gelgel and proclaimed himself Raja. But, in 1705, assisted by the Rajas of Badung and Buleleng, the rightful Raja recovered his throne. In 1710, believing that Gelgel was cursed, the Raja shifted the royal residence to Klungkung.

The gods must have been displeased. By the 1860s, political

power in Bali was focused in the regency of Buleleng, and the Dewa Agung was the supreme ruler in name only. By 1908, the Dutch controlled most of Bali, and their final "acquisition" was to be Klungkung, the residence of the Dewa Agung. Rather than relinquish power, the Dewa Agung and his retinue chose ritual suicide: *puputan*.

Most royal families claim descent from the Gelgel dynasty and today the Gelgel royal family are the most respected family on the island. Alas, little remains of their past glories, as most buildings were razed by the Dutch during the 1908 invasion.

Klungkung is somewhat removed from the tourist rush but has some interesting antiquities. Kerta Gosa, the Court of Justice, located in the former palace at Klungkung, and Goa Lawah, the bat cave temple, are two often-visited attractions.

In the village of **Kamasan**, not far from the town of Klungkung, is a commune of artists who still practise the traditional *wayang* style of painting, derived from the shadow puppets (*wayang kulit*). The village is definitely worth a visit.

KLUNGKUNG TOWN

Klungkung, the town, is the capital of Klungkung, the regency. Despite the historical attractions, Klungkung town does not cater to visitors. The few losmen, mainly frequented by businessmen, are not worth mentioning. There are **two restaurants,** but the night market, **Pasar Senggol** (at the bemo station), has a   good variety of food, and is highly recommended.

Pasar Klungkung, the day market, is one of the best on the island, because the harbour nearby is a major port of call between Java and Lombok. The market is located on the main road (Jl. Diponegoro), and is held every three days, falling on the Balinese day known as *pasah*. The market, as well as the souvenir stalls nearby, often sell fabrics and crafts not available elsewhere in Bali. Fine embroidered *songket*, cheaper than anywhere else on the island, is definitely worth purchasing. The Handicraft Promotion Centre, opposite the Kerta Gosa, also sells crafts. There are quite a few antique shops on the main road, but they mostly sell reproductions.

HOW TO GET THERE

The **bemo station at Klungkung** is a major stop for buses travelling to Besakih (21km - 13 miles), Penelokan (40km - 25 miles), Pandangbai, and Candi Dasa (24km - 15 miles).

Bemos to Besakih and points east, cost Rp800, but tourist prices are gaining favour; and **most bemos do not run after 4pm**. Klungkung town is situated 40km (24 miles) from Denpasar and 13km (9 miles) east of Gianyar.

SIGHTSEEING

The Palace Complex

Kerta Gosa, the royal **Court of Justice**, was built under the watchful eye of the Dewa Agung, Gusti Sideman. An ornate *bale* (open pavilion), it lies in the far-eastern corner of the complex, almost on top of the town's main intersection. Perhaps it served as a warning to passers-by. The elaborately painted ceiling of the Kerta Gosa has traditional *wayang*-style murals in red, gold and black. The scenes depict the heinous punishments of criminals, for instance: an unfaithful woman has her offending parts burnt; a bachelor is attacked by a wild boar; miscreants are boiled to death; and a childless woman is forced to suckle a monstrous caterpillar. Then there are scenes of the afterlife, with the virtuous reigning in the heavens. Indeed, the scenes tell a multitude of stories focusing on fate and divine intervention. The roof of the Kerta Gosa is meticulously maintained, and was last repainted in the 1960s.

The Court of Justice heard only important cases, such as murder or treason, and three *pedanda* presided over the hearings. The judges probably sat in the *bale* in gilt chairs, looking towards the ceiling for inspiration. The court was active until the 1950s when the assembly was moved.

The Bale Kambang, or **Floating Pavilion**, was originally used as a reception hall for visitors, and was completely reconstructed in the 1940s. The *bale* "floats" on a moat, surrounded by stone carvings of figures from the *Mahabharata*. The ceiling also has illustrations, some from Balinese astrology, others depicting Balinese myths. One such story called *Sang Sutasoma*, tells of the trials and tribulations of a family of eighteen children, while the story of *Pan Bryut*, espouses the virtues of the wise man, Pan. Beyond the pavilion is the ornate gateway to the former palace.

OUTLYING ATTRACTIONS

Kamasan

A few kilometres south of Klungkung lies the village of Kamasan, renowned for its **co-operative of artists** who still practise the traditional *wayang* style of painting. Known as the Kamasan style, the figures are stylised, with faces drawn in three-quarters, rather than frontal or profile. There is no perspective, as such, and subjects of importance are painted in the centre, with gods at the top, and evil spirits at the bottom. The ceiling of the Kerta Gosa is a typical *wayang* depiction. Originally, the paintings were drawn on cotton, wood or paper, with a palm-leaf quill filled with soot; then, natural dyes were applied with bamboo brushes to colour the figures. These days, most painters use acrylics and ink on canvas. Although Western conventions demand a single artist, painting was, and in many cases still is, a joint effort. The master painter plans the themes and layout of the painting, and then directs the apprentices in the colouring of the figures. Finally, the master outlines the figures in ink, occasionally enhancing details with gold paint.

Although wealthy Indonesians and Westerners commission paintings, sadly, most painters are impoverished, and the government fears that this traditional style may die out. The artists in Kamasan are all willing to demonstrate their techniques and appreciate Western patronage.

Gelgel

About four kilometres (2.5 miles) south of Klungkung is the former Court of Gelgel, the once magnificent and powerful capital of the Gelgel kingdom. The first Raja built the palace in 1515, and it remained the political centre until the courtly retinue moved to Klungkung. The only vestiges of past glory can be found in the ruins of the sacred Pura Jero Agung or "Great Palace Temple", and the remnants of the second largest palace in Gelgel, Pura Jero Kapal. To the east, is Pura Dasar, a state temple built as an adjunct to the "Mother Temple" at Besakih.

Goa Lawah

The celebrated "Bat Cave", as its name implies, almost pulsates with thousands of flapping, squealing, fruit bats. A temple guards the entrance to the sacred cave from malign spirits and intruders, but even the most intrepid or stupid would not dare enter, for the cavern and everything nearby is covered by a blanket of excrement. The cave was found by the priest Empu Kuturan, and supposedly extends to Pura Goa, the "cave temple", at the Besakih complex. Legend has it that a huge snake, Naga Basuki, resides in the cavity, living on a seemingly infinite supply of bats.

Admission Rp500 and temple dress is required.

NUSA PENIDA

Few tourists venture to Nusa Penida. An arid, limestone island it was, until recently bereft of vegetation, except for the odd cactus. Once thought to be inhabited by malign spirits, the Balinese still believe that all diseases hail from Nusa Penida. The home of Jero Gede Macaling, the mythical giant, Nusa Penida became the last abode of reprobates, criminals, and seditious subjects banished from Gelgel. Today, it seems a sinister ambience still haunts the island.

Thanks to government grants, limited cultivation is possible, and irrigation systems utilise the rainfall that previously seeped into underground caverns. Apart from cassava, corn, coconuts, peanuts and soybeans, little is grown, and rice has to be imported. The economy is largely funded by seaweed farming, and dried seaweed is exported to Hong Kong, Singapore, Japan and France, for the manufacture of cosmetics, as well as agar-agar, a thickening agent for cooking.

This is definitely not a tourist resort - few people speak English, the roads are treacherous, and tourist accommodation is almost non-existent. But Nusa Penida and the surrounding islands offer good swimming, surfing, snorkelling, and scuba diving.

Located in Badung Strait between Bali and Lombok, the island is 20km by 16km (12 miles x 10 miles) rising to a height of 529m (1735ft) at Bukit Mundi. Nusa Penida along with the satellite islands of Nusa Lembongan and Nusa Ceningan make up Bali's three "sister islands". A counterpoint to the lush mainland, Nusa Penida is more like the Bukit Peninsula which is also a limestone formation. Exotic fauna abound — some surprisingly reminiscent of Australian wildlife — including the rare Rothschild's mynah bird.

HOW TO GET THERE

Transport to the three islands is available from Padangbai and Kusamba in the east, or from Sanur and Benoa in the south. Most boats leave at 7am, and the choppy straits and severe winds can make for an arduous journey — cover all valuables with plastic as most boats are open. Different boats travel to different destinations, but bemos on the islands meet all of them, so it doesn't really matter where you disembark.

The easiest way to arrange transport to the islands is through travel agents, but here's how to do it yourself.

From Kusamba

About 200m from the market, outriggers carry passengers to either Jungutbatu on Nusa Lembongan, or to Toyapakeh on Nusa Penida. Another port in Kusamba, down Jl. Pair Putih (towards Amlapura), has bigger boats. The crossing is about 14km (9 miles) from Kusamba to Nusa Lembongan, and the journey from either point takes about two to three hours (Rp5000 one way). Boats leave when they are full so departure times vary. Boats can be chartered from both harbours - a round trip starts from Rp50,000 (depending on the boat size).

From Padangbai

The best alternative is to take a "speed" boat and they leave at about 7am. The fare is slightly higher than from Kusamba, but the journey is considerably faster - about 50 minutes. The boat arrives at Buyuk, which is close to Samalan.

From Sanur

Traditional outriggers (prahu) can be hired from near the Natour Grand Bali Beach Hotel. There is no regular service and the price is negotiable. The journey takes over two hours (less on the return journey). If intending a day trip, leave early in the morning because the skippers do not like travelling through Badung Strait in the late afternoon.

From Benoa

The most pleasurable means of travelling to Nusa Lembongan is by hiring a yacht from Benoa. Tour Devco (ph 31 591) has day trips for $US60, and will organise transport to and from your hotel.

ACCOMMODATION

The main village on the island is Sampalan. The only accommodation is the very cheap losmen-style, *Bungalows Pemda*, which are at the eastern end of the village. Of course there is no restaurant, but there are warungs.

LOCAL TRANSPORT
In Nusa Penida the boats arrive at Buyuk or Toyapakeh. Bemos run from both ports to Sampalan, and run irregularly between villages. Charter a bemo around the island for Rp20,000 an hour.

SIGHTSEEING
Tourism has not reached Nusa Penida and everywhere are authentic unspoilt sights. Temples, as on the mainland, are ubiquitous, but tend to be simpler in design.

Goa Karangsari
You'll probably have to hitch a ride on a goods truck and most carry passengers for a fee. Take the coast road east from Sampalan. The cave is past Karangsari but before Sewena. Say "goa" (cave), and the truck driver will stop there.

Disembark at the warung and hire a guide (about Rp6000). Although the guide will have a kerosene lamp, take a strong torch to see the shrine and bats. The entrance is small but the cave itself is huge and side passages lead nowhere. The cave emerges at the other side of the hill.

Pura Peed
From Sampalan, take the road west for a ten-minute journey to the village of Peed. On the right side of the road is the limestone temple dedicated to the malicious giant, Jero Gede Macaling. The temple's architecture features monstrous and hideous statues, and nearby a gruesome mouth gapes from the trunk of a gnarled tree. Worshippers come here to placate the awesome figure, who they believe responsible for unleashing evil forces.

NUSA LEMBONGAN
Most travellers that visit this small island arrive with

surfboard in tow. But Nusa Lembogan is simply a quiet retreat. There are no bemos, and in fact, no traffic. However, there are a few restaurants and a selection of losmen. Like Nusa Penida, the island derives its main source of income from seaweed farming. Bird watchers (the feathered kind) will be fascinated with the exotic bird life. There are also great views of south Bali, especially at night.

Marine Sports
The surfing is fabulous.
A perfect right breaks over a coral encrusted shipwreck - the "wreck". "Lacerations" and the "playground" are also much lauded breaks, and an outrigger can be hired to travel between them. **See the surfing section in the "Travel Information" section.**

The small channel between Nusa Lembongan and Nusa Ceningan is a very good spot for snorkelling - the water is crystal clear and visibility is very good. Snorkelling gear can be hired on the island for Rp8000 per day, but scuba gear has to be hired in Sanur.

For information on "How to get There" see the same in the section on Nusa Penida.

```
NOTES



```

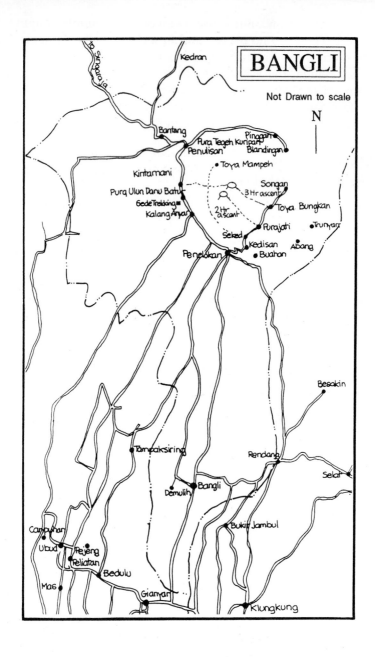

BANGLI

The landlocked and mountainous regency of Bangli includes some of the most magnificent scenery on the island. Luminous green rice fields cover the undulating land, and the revered Gunung Batur (1717m - 5633ft), a still active volcano, dominates the landscape. The placid Lake Batur rests in a huge crater, overshadowed by Batur, and the lesser-known but higher, Gunung Abang (2152m - 7060ft). In the morning, tourists visit the towns of Kintamani and Penelokan to observe the imposing Batur before clouds descend to obscure the mountain. The afternoon panorama is as splendid as the morning, enhanced by the eerie atmosphere of mysterious clouds. Little wonder that locals speak in hushed tones of black magic.

The main road through the regency of Bangli starts east of Gianyar, passes through the town of Bangli, and climbs to Penelokan, then Kintamani. Past the town of Bangli, the road ascends and the picturesque rice fields diminish, replaced by ashen, volcanic terrain. Vegetation is sparse, it's much cooler, and you know the altitude is high because your ears have popped. The route from Penelokan to Kintamani follows the mountainous crater of an ancient, extinct volcano that surrounds Gunung Batur.

BANGLI TOWN

The capital of the regency of the same name, Bangli, is a sleepy, little village. About 40km (25 miles) from Denpasar, via Gianyar, Bangli was once the site of a royal court. It is said that the Dewa Agung of Klungkung ordered his son to find the "auspicious red forest". The prince did, and "Bangli", which means the "red forest", became his kingdom. For a time, Bangli was annexed by the king of Karangasem, and later in 1849, it was colonised by the Dutch.

Bangli is home to the only psychiatric hospital on the island, the source of much mirth to non-Bangliites. Bangli is also known for its "black" and "white" magic, and many trance healers, known as *balian*, are sought by Balinese from all over the island. There are eight royal palaces spread around the town, and the most notable is the Puri Denpasar palace. Fully restored, the palace also operates as a hotel, managed by the late king's grandson.

Pura Kehen

Pura Kehen, the beautiful state temple of Bangli, lies north-east of the centre of town. Three copper pillars indicate that the temple was built in the 11th century, and the animistic motifs incorporated in the carvings suggest pre-Majapahit architecture. There are eight courtyards and 43 altars climbing to the sacred inner *jeroan*, which houses an 11-tiered *meru* tower. A sprawling complex of temples and shrines, the site resembles the impressive network found at the "Mother Temple" in Besakih. A huge staircase lined with dancing *wayang* figures leads to a gateway known ominously as the "Great Exit". Notice the customary *kulkul* drum perched in a *banyan* tree, and the not so customary Chinese porcelain which adorns the walls of the outer courtyard. If in Bali at the time of the Pura Kehen's anniversary festival (*odalan*), be sure not to miss the unrivalled spectacle. As the year is 210 days, the date of the festival differs each year. The tourist offices in Kuta and Denpasar will happily supply calendars of events for the month.

Not far from Pura Kehen is the **Wisata Budaya Art Centre**. One of the biggest art centres on Bali, it houses an excellent exhibition which surpasses displays found elsewhere on the island. The centre also hosts several different local *barong* performances.

GUNUNG BATUR AND LAKE BATUR

Penelokan

Driving up to Gunung Batur on the Bangli road, Penelokan is the first village on the crater rim. Penelokan, which means "lookout" has spectacular views — stay awhile and contemplate the serene majesty of this mountain. Effectively, what you're admiring is the cavernous remains of a massive volcano, probably bigger than Agung, that erupted thousands of years ago, bursting the entire cone and leaving only the hollow rim on which you're standing.

A quick word about Penelokan, the hawkers are insufferable. The minute you open the door of your car, mobs of men, women and children will bombard you with the usual garish garudas and tawdry temple-sashes. Eat lunch, enjoy the view, then scoot.

GUNUNG BATUR

In the crater of a once gargantuan volcano stands the blackened cone of Gunung Batur. This sacred volcano, second only to Gunung Agung, is still active. Batur erupted in 1917, again in 1927, when it completely destroyed the village of Batur, and further activity occurred when Agung erupted in 1963. Batur has two craters and its slopes are blemished from lava flows, particularly on the eastern side adjacent to the lake. The cone is 1717m (5633ft) high, and the crater in which it sits is 11km (7 miles) in diameter and 183m (600ft) deep.

The Ascent of Batur

Guides can be contacted at Gede's Trekking, just near the market at Kintamani; alternatively, many of the losmen organise treks. Although most climbs take about three hours up and less than two hours down, make an early start (around 6am) as the afternoon heat can be exhausting. Don't even think about climbing during the wet season.

There are **two tracks** favoured by visitors: one starts from Toya Bungkah (a three-hour climb to the second crater); and the other begins at Purajati (a two-hour climb to the first crater). Both paths are well signposted and are frequented by young locals selling drinks.

Public bemos run from Penelokan to Kedisan for around Rp700, then to Purajati for Rp400. The walk from Penelokan to Kedisan takes about 45 minutes.

LAKE BATUR

Danau Batur is the biggest lake in Bali. Set in the monstrous crater next to Batur, the lake is over 7.5km (5 miles) long, 2.5km (1.5 miles) wide, 70m (230ft) deep, and lies 1031m (3383ft) above sea level. To the west of the lake is desolate lava rock and to the east, are the lush slopes of Gunung Abang (2152m - 7060ft), the second highest mountain in Bali.

Around the Lake

From Penelokan, take the road that zigzags down the crater to the lakeside village of Kedisan. At the bottom of the road, turn right to hire boats across the lake; or turn left to the villages of Toya Bungkah and Songan (this road also meanders to the bubbling hot springs known as Air Panas).

Trunyan

This famous Bali Aga village can be reached by boat from Kedisan. The arts and customs of the people of Trunyan predate Hindu times and their social tenets are unique. The one thing for which they're famous is that their dead are not cremated but are left to decompose beneath a tree.

Those adventurous enough to hire a boat to Trunyan are in for a real treat. The moment happy travellers disembark, locals besiege them to pay money for simply stepping on land! Then, a guide must be purchased as an escort to the temple, fending off beggars and ignoring the scowls of villagers along the way, to farewell a couple of thousand rupiah to walk around the temple — few are permitted entrance — and told that the biggest statue on the island, the 4m (13ft) high, Dewa Ratu Gede Pancering Jagat ("god who is the centre of the world"), the statue you've paid rupiah to see, is hidden in a shrine. Lots more rupiah will be handed over by intrepid statue viewers, but they'll die wondering if it is indeed 4m high. Then it's in the boat again to view (without fear or favour) the long-awaited cemetery. All this to see a rotten skull or two. There's not a putrefying body in sight! Naturally, the villagers conceal the real cemetery from intruders. Then it's back to the boat for an argument with the licensed bandit with a boat (boatman) because he has increased the price of the fare and you've already paid! Why bother? As you can see it was not one of my most enjoyable experiences.

BATUR

The original village and temple of Batur were built on the lake's shore, but following the eruption in 1917, the entire village was devastated and a thousand lives were lost. Surprisingly, the lava flows ceased at the gate of the temple and the Balinese felt that they should rebuild the village due to the propitious omen. When Batur erupted again, in 1926, the temple was also devastated, but the *meru* shrine to the goddess of the lake survived. The people finally gave up, and the entire village moved to the rim of the crater, just before Kintamani. The temple was dismantled and relocated on the rim, which must have been a logistical nightmare. The temple, Pura Ulun Danur Batur, is a complex of nine temples which are slowly increasing in number. Here, deference is paid to Dewi Ulun Danu, goddess of the lake, and her shrine, an 11-tiered *meru* tower, is in the main temple.

KINTAMANI

Most visitors take a day tour to Kintamani, spending time in one of the various restaurants that are huddled on the outer rim of an ancient volcano. The food buffet-style is invariably lukewarm, but all the establishments have superb vantage points.

A tiny market village, Kintamani is 1500m (4921ft) above sea level. Palm-leaf (lontar) and stone inscriptions suggest that the village precedes the Majapahit empire, and the many surrounding villages claim to be "Bali Aga" or indigenous Balinese.

HOW TO GET THERE

By Bemo

From Denpasar's Kerengeng terminal, take a bemo to Bangli (Rp1000) via Klunkung, then to Penelokan (Rp600).

From Ubud, take a bemo to Sakah (Rp400), then to Gianyar (Rp800), then to Penelokan (Rp1000).

From Singaraja a minibus costs Rp1500.

By Car

Kintamani is 68km (42 miles) from Denpasar; 75 km (47 miles) from Kuta; 41km (25 miles) from Gianyar; and 52km (32 miles) from Singaraja.

TOURS

Tours can be arranged at Kuta, Sanur, Ubud, Candi Dasa and other places. Prices differ according to the number of passengers and the route taken — shop around to get the best price for what you want to see. From the south, the route generally taken is via Ubud and Tampaksiring, stopping at Goa Gajah and Tirta Empul. A less-frequented route (the road is narrow and pot-holed) passes through Ubud and the villages of Tegallalang, Sebatu and Pujung.

ACCOMMODATION

Prices range from around US$4 a night to US$20. At night it gets damnably cold so take a blanket and a jumper. The accommodation is more or less losmen-style, which means it's very spartan, but cheap. Most hotels have great views, but lack hot water. There are no telephones, nor airconditioning. Check them out for yourself.

Two hotels recommended are:

Hotel Puri Astina. Kintamani, north of the market. Four of the rooms are quite big and have great views. Room $20.

Lakeview Restaurant and Homestay. Penelokan. Very basic but fabulous views. Room $9-$11.

EATING OUT

Many of the losmen have warungs attached. There are a few warungs in Kintamani, but most of the larger restaurants cater to the day tour lunch crowd and serve buffets - avoid them.

Lakeview. Penelokan. Open for lunch and dinner, and offers a variety of dishes.

Batur Garden Restaurant. Chinese and Indonesian. Open for lunch only.

Rumah Makan Cahaya. North Kintamani. One of the nicest warungs in Kintamani. Good food and nice atmosphere.

 NOTES.

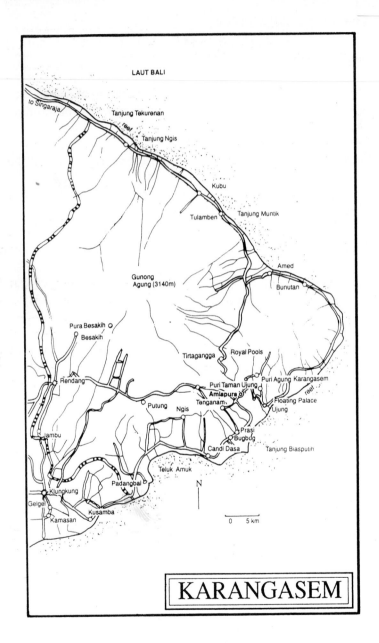

LAUT BALI

to Singaraja

reef

Tanjung Tekurenan

Tanjung Ngis

Kubu

Tulamben   Tanjung Muntik

Amed

Gunong
Agung (3140m)   Bunutan

Pura Besakih

Besakih

Tirtagangga   Royal Pools

Rendang   Puri Taman Ujung   Puri Agung Karangasem

Amlapura   reef

Putung   Ngis   Tenganam   Floating Palace

Ujung

Jambu   Prasi

Bugbug

Candi Dasa   Tanjung Biasputih

Teluk Amuk   N

Padangbai

Klungkung

Gelgel   Kusamba   0   5 km

Kamasan

KARANGASEM

KARANGASEM

The regency of Karangasem is unrivalled in beauty. The diversity of Bali's landscape offers wonders to behold, but in Karangasem, the contrasts are intensified. In the highlands, impeccably terraced hills affording views to the sea are set against black rivers of volcanic ash, and large, stupa-like rocks. Such scenery could only be dwarfed by the colossal presence of Gunung Agung. And on the slopes of this, Bali's most sacred mountain, lies the sprawling complex of temples, the "Mother Temple".

Karangasem has not experienced the whirlwind developments of the other regencies, and has changed little. For instance, the "language of courtesies" is still prevalent, and many old dances and rituals have persisted unchanged. **Candi Dasa**, the only resort in the regency, is sedate compared to its counterparts in the south. Indeed, who could blame such conservatism, when plainly, one imagines the gods must sit upon Gunung Agung, watching every move the people make.

History

When the Majapahit descendant, Dewa Agung of Klungkung, divided Bali in the 16th century, he ruled the regency of Karangasem through a regent. But, as time passed, the regency claimed more independence, until in the early 18th century Karangasem attained enough power to colonise Lombok and Sumbawa. Alas, in 1894, the tables turned and the Dutch "removed" the Balinese rulers from Lombok and soon after invaded Karangasem. The Raja, Agung Anglurah Ketut, retained limited power, and managed to commission several lavish, even ostentatious, palaces.

Amlapura, a bustling little village, is the capital. The regency derives much of its economy from farming rice, coffee and cloves, as well as fishing and salt-panning.

PADANGBAI

A small Muslim village, it is also Bali's eastern-most port. The occasional cruiser and yacht moors here, and it is also the terminal for the ferry to Lombok, which departs three times a day. The trip takes three hours and costs from Rp8000-Rp12000.

Cornelius De Houtman stopped here and was so enamoured of the land that he called it "Young Holland". Padangbai is a quiet little village, until the ferry arrives and the hawkers scurry out of the woodwork to annoy the visitors. Then the ferry disappears, and there's peace again.

TENGANAN

Before you reach Candi Dasa, a road branching off to the left leads to the village of Tenganan, the home of the *Bali Aga*, the "original Balinese". An ordered and prosperous village, it is the antithesis of Trunyan, the "Bali Aga" village at Lake Batur. The descendants of Tenganan settled in Bali long before the Hindu Majapahit Empire called Bali home, and the village traces its origins to a holy chronicle known as the *Usana Bali*. According to the text, the ancestors of the Tengananese where chosen by their creator, Batara Indra, to perpetuate the rituals and ceremonies passed to them from the gods. Furthermore, the sacred lands granted to the ancestors were to be administered by the people of Tenganan, and kept free from impurity. Life in this exclusive and cloistered village is devoted to maintaining the divine order, and to following the traditional law (*adat*) to the letter.

Tenganan is possibly the only village on the island that still maintains a communal way of life, and all homes and property are owned by the village. The rice fields are tended by exiles (who live outside the compound) or by neighbouring villagers who receive half the yield in payment. Consequently, the village is quite wealthy and its residents have much time to dedicate to the arts.

The people of Tenganan are famed for their expertise in creating *geringsing* cloth, by the technique known as double *ikat*. The *ikat* method involves selectively dyeing threads prior to weaving by binding them in groups, so that the threads will not absorb colour when dipped in a dyebath. The process is repeated, adding different colours to the thread. In south Bali, only the weft is bound, but the double *ikat* process dyes both the warp and the weft. This makes weaving the threads extremely difficult, as the tension of the threads must be exact so that the patterns on both threads match. It is said that *Geringsing* was taught to the Tengananese by Batara Indra, and that the cloth protects the wearer from malign spirits.

Before Candi Dasa became a burgeoning resort, Tenganan was inaccessible and virtually isolated; now a sealed road connects the village with the outside world. Protected by natural boundaries and walls, the immaculate village is 500m by 250m (1640ft x 820ft), and has four impressive gateways located at the cardinal points. Three parallel roads run downhill, north to south, aligned with Gunung Agung and the sea, and the dwellings are set in parallel rows of nearly identical brick and mortar boxes. The village is a microcosm of 13th century, pre-Hindu life — except for the odd television antenna impaled on a thatched roof.

Tenganan is also famous for its three-day *Udaba Sambah* festival, which is held every six months. The unmarried girls of the village, ceremonially adorned, participate in a ritual to unite the earth with the heavens. They sit atop a huge wooden frame, not unlike a ferris wheel, displaying their charms. The young men engage in a man-to-man combat ritual, armed with spiky pandanus leaves, to the accompaniment of the haunting tones of the ancient *gamelan*. Tenganan has its own *gamelan*, the *gong selunding*, which is unique to the village.

CANDI DASA

A developing, yet relatively unspoilt tourist resort, Candi Dasa (pronounced "chandy"), is the perfect place to stop for a while to explore the environs. A nice escape from the south, the restaurants and hotels are very good, and the night life isn't bad either. The locals are also more relaxed, with few soliciting travellers to buy, buy, buy. In fact, Candi Dasa has some of Kuta's virtues, without all the vices.

Candi Dasa means "ten temples" and although there are not ten temples, the village shrine has a ten-tiered gateway, one of the few shrines to use even-numbered symbolism. Perched high above the palm-fringed lagoon, the temple offers superb views of the beach.

The white coral sand beaches, calm water and colourful sea-life make Candi Dasa a lovely sea resort. The problem is that the sea is fast encroaching on the beach, which at high tide is barely visible. A huge wall has been built between the main road and the coast to enable the construction of tourist facilities, and huge cement breakwaters attempt to combat erosion. Popular opinion though, holds that rather than stopping the erosion, they are actually aggravating it.

HOW TO GET THERE

By Bemo

Bemos depart from Denpasar's Kerengeng terminal for Candi Dasa and cost Rp3000 (although tourist prices are becoming popular).
From Klunkung and Amlapura, bemos leave frequently and the fare is Rp500.

By Hiring a Bemo

Depending on the number of travellers, the season etc, four

people can charter a private bemo from Kuta for about Rp20000.

By Car

Candi Dasa is 13km (8 miles) south-west of Amlapura; 25km (16 miles) from Klunkung; 38km (24 miles) from Gianyar; 69km (43 miles) from Denpasar; and 78km (48 miles) from Kuta.

ACCOMMODATION

Although Candi Dasa is small, it has a good selection of hotels. Prices based on one night's accommodation are in US$, and should be used as a guide only. The telephone code is 0361.

Rama Ocean View Bungalows, Ph 251 864. Located about a kilometre out of town, a beautiful hotel, but difficult to travel to, and from, Candi Dasa by night (the transport may improve). Pool, great restaurant, fitness centre, games room, videos, hot water and airconditioning. Room $60-$80, plus 15.5% tax & service charges.

Candi Dasa Beach Bungalows II, Ph 235 539. The best hotel in terms of location, it's set in the middle of the village, with a beachfront position. Bungalows, they are not, rather a two-storey cement monstrosity. All rooms have a balcony or verandah, hot water and airconditioning. Room $30-$40 includes 15.5% tax and service charges.

The Water Garden, ph 235 540. 12 rooms. Across the road from the beach, individual, charming cottages are set in beautiful gardens, and there's a pool and restaurant. Room $60-$65, plus 15.5% tax and service charges.

Bali Sumdra Indah Hotel, Ph 235 542. 56 rooms. Great location with a good restaurant, and a pool with a sunken bar. Excellent value for money. Hot water and airconditioning.

Candi Dasa also has the best losmen-style accommodation on the island, try the Amlapura end of town. Depending on the season, prices are often negotiable.

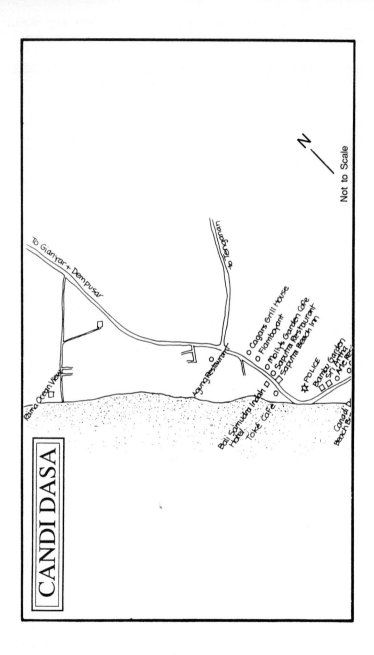

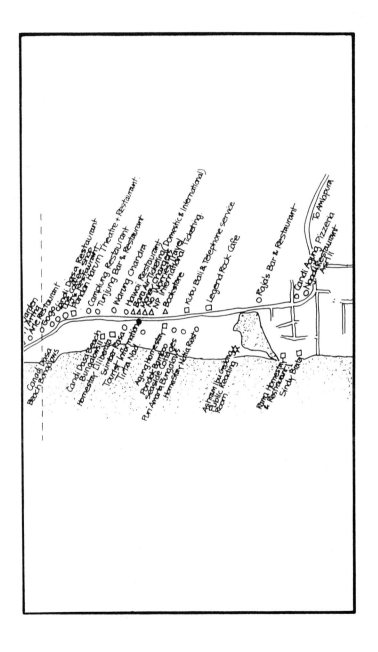

Room $20-$40.

Here are a few:

Losmen Gerinsing. A bargain! Secluded beachfront position with brick bungalows. Room Rp8500-Rp15,000.

Pondok Bambu. Beachfront and very comfortable. Room Rp7000-Rp10,000.

Satria. Close to the beach. Room Rp7000-Rp10,000.

EATING OUT

Puri Bagus Beach Hotel's restaurant. Probably the best and most expensive restaurant in town — but worth it.

Camplung. Open for big, hearty breakfasts, or for the best chilli prawns in town.

Flamboyant. Tenganan end of town. Very reasonably priced and possesses the only billiard table for miles.

Molly's. Good coffee and cakes.

Pandan Restaurant. On the beach, renowned for its Indonesian and Chinese fare.

Pizzeria Candi Agung. For those that yearn for pizza.

Pondok Bambo Restaurant.

Tirta Nadi Restaurant & Bar. Lots of good seafood and surprisingly good steaks. Stays open till late.

TJ's Cafe. Second-best when compared to its namesake in Kuta, but similar menu. Pond and miniature falls complement the balmy atmosphere.

ENTERTAINMENT

The Beer Garden. At the time of writing, the Beer Garden was **the** place to go, thriving until the wee hours.

Candi Dasa Beach Bungalows II. *Barong* and *Kris* held weekly, inquire at the hotel.

Go-Go's. Dancing and drinking for the young and hip.

Pandan Harum. Dance performances most nights. Rp5000.

SHOPPING

Candi Dasa is not a shopper's paradise, in fact if you're after clothing, jewellery, or carvings, forget it.

The Bookstore, on the main road, has a wide range of titles on Bali and Indonesia, and also sells good maps.

For general merchandise, Asri Shop has two stores (in the middle of town, and also out of town towards Amlapura).

MISCELLANEOUS

Doctors

Two doctors are available at limited times. Inquire at the Candi Dasa Beach Bungalows II.

MG International Air Ticketing

Can arrange air tickets for Garuda, Qantas, Singapore Airlines and many others.

Money Changers

There are several money changers although the rate is not comparable with Kuta. Shop around.

Photo Developers

There are two one-hour developers.

WATER ACTIVITIES

Candi Dasa beach is great for snorkelling and diving, but not for surfing. A couple of hundred metres from the shore, near the breakers, is a snorkelling wonderland. A dazzling selection of multicoloured fish darting in and out of labyrinths of coral, will entertain you for hours.

Most of the hotels rent snorkelling gear. For scuba gear see the Stingray Dive Centre at the Bali Samudra Indah Hotel or the Bali Dive Centre in the Candi Dasa Beach Bungalows II. Both offer diving in various places around the island, and prices are from US$40.

OUTLYING ATTRACTIONS

Amlapura

In times past, Amlapura was the capital of an affluent kingdom — now it is a weary little village. Once called Karangasem, its name was changed according to local legend to confuse malevolent spirits who orchestrated the eruptions of Gunung Agung — the bane of Karangasem. But to no avail, for in 1963, the town was again devastated by an outburst from the volcano. Lava never reached the town, but the attendant earthquakes and whirlwinds resulted in its complete isolation for three years. A huge lava flow is evident when entering the town from the south.

The last Raja of Karangasem, Agung Anglurah Ketut, built several water palaces worth visiting for their eccentric grandeur.

Puri Kanginan

The famous residence of the late raja was built early this century. Slowly decaying, the palace is a whimsical mishmash of Balinese, Chinese and European architectural designs. You may notice the *Bale London* which derives its name from an English-looking crest that decorates much of the furniture. The palace is still inhabited by some of the raja's wives and his descendants, but visitors are welcome, even for the night (Rp15,000).

Admission Rp500.

Ujung Water Palace

Three kilometres out of Karangasem is the first of the Raja's water palaces. Built in the early 1920s, the magnificent and stately residence is set amidst green terraces and placid ponds. A conjured vision: the palace is no more and all that remains after the eruption of Gunung Agung in 1963 are a huge pool and a few statues and portals — woeful vestiges of a once great palace.

Ujung is 4km (2 miles) south of Amlapura and a bemo to Ujung from the Amlapura terminal costs about Rp500.

Tirtagangga

On the slopes of Gunung Agung lies the second water palace, Tirtagangga. The name means "water of the Ganges" and commemorates the Hindu's sacred river. Built in 1947, on the site of a natural spring, the landscape and fountains make this a fine place to enjoy the salubrious pools. Although in dire need of restoration, the complex of pools is now open for public use. Enjoy lunch in the warung above the palace, or stay overnight in the Tirta Ayu homestay.

About 6km (4 miles) north-west of Amlapura, a bemo costs Rp700. Admission is Rp500 and Rp300 to use the pools.

THE MOTHER TEMPLE

The most sacred temple in all of Bali, Pura Besakih or the "Mother temple", graces the slopes of the venerated Gunung Agung. The temple is considered the essence of divine powers on Bali, and it is a state temple, a shrine for all Balinese. Thousands upon thousands of pilgrims visit annually. Gunung Agung is the tallest mountain on Bali (3014m - 9888ft), and the temple is nearly 1000m (3280ft) above sea level. Arrive before 9am, because Gunung Agung is often veiled in clouds by mid morning.

The name, "Mother Temple", is misleading as there is not a single temple, but a complex of 22 temples meandering up the mountainside. In prehistoric times, the auspicious Gunung Agung was probably the site of a terraced sanctuary where animistic cults worshipped the god of the volcano. When the Majapahit Empire established itself at Gelgel, the Dewa Agung appropriated the sanctuary transforming it into a Hindu temple for the entire island. Pura Besakih retained the distinction even when the court shifted from Gelgel to Klungkung, and since those times, the complex has gradually increased.

At first sight, the temple complex appears a confusion of shrines. Nonetheless, the complex has a tripartite design which venerates the holy trinity of Siwa, Brahma and Wisnu. Additional shrines are located throughout the compound, representing all the regencies, as well as the entire pantheon of Hindu gods and ancestral deities. Pura Penataran Agung, "the Great Temple of State" is the symbolic centre of the Besakih complex and is a shrine to Siwa. Pura Kiduling Kreteg, the "temple south of the bridge" honours Brahma, while Pura Batu Madeg, the "temple of the standing stone" is dedicated to Wisnu. The longitudinal axis of these temples faces *kaja* (north), to the peak of the great Agung.

Pura Penataran Agung

At the top of some 50 steps is the split gate, or *candi bentar*, which opens onto the main courtyard. The courtyard has over 50 shrines half of which represent deities. A forest of *meru* towers (the more tiers, the higher the god), is impressive, but unlike most Balinese shrines, those in the Besakih complex are bereft of colour and ornate carvings.

The lotus throne or *padmasana* dates from the 17th century, and is the symbolic centre of the entire complex. The three seats of the temple are dedicated to Wisnu (left), Siwa (centre) and Brahma (right). During festivals, the seats are enshrined with cloth: black for Wisnu, white for Siwa and red for Brahma. Most of the structures in the temple were built after the earthquake of 1917. Unfortunately, visitors are not permitted in this temple, but a climb above the courtyards enables views of the many shrines and statuary, as well as the coastline.

Festivals

Bhatara Turun Kabeh

An annual festival, celebrated on the full moon of the tenth lunar month (in March or April) is the time when the "gods descend together", a basic traslation of the name of the month-long festival. Conducted by Brahman priests, it is the most important ritual in the Balinese calender.

There are, in fact, over 70 rituals held each year, most of which are held by Besakih's own priests.

Eka Dasa Rudra

The most important ritual celebration in Bali, the Eka Dasa Rudra is celebrated every hundred years to purify the cosmos and placate Rudra, the merciless manifestation of Siwa.

In 1963, amidst political turmoil, Bali prepared itself for the most important ritual of the century. President Sukarno had invited many international guests, and although smoke and steam were issuing from the mountain during February, the government continued with preparations despite warnings from religious leaders. On March 12, Gunung Agung exploded. The mountain erupted with such force that much of the temple complex was destroyed. Fatalities reached 1600, crops were destroyed, over 50 villages were ruined, and huge ominous, black clouds covered east Java. Thousands of people were evacuated to Sulawesi. Today, there is little evidence of the destruction except for the blackened countryside north-east of Klungkung.

Eka Dasa Rudra was held again in 1979 on a propitious date, and the mother mountain was serene throughout.

Maintenance of the Complex

Originally, the Dewa Agung was responsible for the temple through vassal princes, and even when the Dutch took over, the arrangement continued. The only regency that has not been designated temples to maintain is Tabanan, because it has its own state temple, Pura Luhur. Since 1979, and the successful *Eka Dasa Rudra*, Besakih is considered to be **the** Hindu temple in Indonesia, and consequently is partly funded by the Indonesian government.

Admission is by donation and is recorded in a log.

Suspiciously, there are no donations under a couple of thousand rupiah — one suspects that a nought is added here or there. But, given that all donations fund the temple, and this is Bali's temple, a couple of dollars is little price to pay for hours spent wandering through the maze of Hindu shrines. After paying admission, visitors are besieged by tour guides offering their services — you'd be wise to take a guide, but negotiate the price before leaving. The complex is huge, and three hours can easily pass walking amongst these wondrous shrines. And remember to wear sensible walking shoes.

GUNUNG AGUNG

All roads lead to Gunung Agung - metaphorically, perhaps. The most sacred of mountains, it is also an active volcano. The Balinese regard the "Great Mountain" as the "navel of the world" and the basis of the *kaja - kelod* axis. Everything that is holy faces towards the mountain or *kaja*, while everything that is evil points towards the sea or *kelod*. The construction of temples and houses obeys this principle, and indeed many people sleep with their heads towards Gunung Agung. The cone of the volcano has an elevation of 3014m (9888ft), and rose to 3142m (10308ft) before the eruption in 1963.

If you want to climb Gunung Agung, a guide is essential, as there are many tracks and it is easy to get lost. Guides wander around the complex at Besakih and are not apprehensive about approaching tourists. The climb is much more difficult than that of Gunung Batur, and takes an entire day. In fact, most leave prepared to camp overnight. The trek should start very early, before 3am on a night with a fullish moon. **Never attempt the climb in the wet season.**

BULELENG

The regency of Buleleng is a narrow band of land across the top of the island of Bali. To the north is the Bali Sea, and to the south, Buleleng shares borders with every regency except Gianyar and Klungkung. The largest regency, it covers an area of 1370 sq km and is isolated from the rest of the island by a chain of volcanoes stretching across the island east to west.

The climate is drier than in south Bali, and wet-rice cultivation is not as extensive; instead, the region is known for its fruit, coffee and clove plantations. In the dry season, the parched red earth splits, the grass withers, and doe-eyed cattle roam amongst fruit trees. Famed for its black sand beaches, natural springs and waterfalls, Buleleng is very different to the south, and that's half the attraction.

Cultural Character

But Buleleng isn't just geographically different to the south. Its physical isolation from the south, coupled with its proximity to the Java Sea and foreign influences, have enabled the regency to develop a distinct cultural character. The regency's intricate style of carving adorns many temples and palaces, and is some of the most stunning sculpture to be found on the island. Many of the dances are more aggressive than those found in the south; the strenuous and frenetic *kebyar* dance originated in Buleleng, as did the suggestive, *joged*. The jazzy *gong kebyar* orchestra was also an innovation of the north, and styles are now featured in the programs of dance performances in the south.

History

During the 17th century, Buleleng reached its political zenith under Gusti Panji Sakti, founder of the regency, who extended his realm by conquering East Java and Karangasem. But power waned under Sakti's grandsons, who were caught off guard when the Raja of Karangasem embarked on a crusade to acquire the throne. In 1823, Buleleng successfully rebelled against Karangasem's authority, but its freedom was fleeting.

The Dutch were also interested in northern Bali, and between 1846 and 1848, made three assaults on Buleleng. The first two proved unsuccessful, but the third saw the largest assembled force ever used in the Archipelago. The Raja of Buleleng, assisted by his brother the Balinese hero Djilantik, fought valiantly against the Dutch, but was finally defeated and died in battle.

In 1849, the raja's family signed an agreement with the Dutch to relinquish power in all but name. The Dutch ruled through a family member, but it wasn't until 1882 that they officially controlled northern Bali. Indeed, the Dutch dominated the north decades before the south, and Dutch influences are more prevalent in Buleleng than anywhere else on the island. Ironically, during colonisation, Singaraja was the capital of Bali, and the gateway to the rest of the world.

Today, many travellers seem to shun Buleleng, unaware of its manifold charms, and the hospitality of its people.

SINGARAJA

Singaraja has experienced successive historical transformations; first as a regal court centre, then as the capital of Dutch commerce in Asia and administration, and finally as a modern district capital. Although it's a modern, bustling city, Singaraja also marks time. Horse-drawn dokars still saunter along the tree-lined streets, and old Chinese shops and markets reflect a colonial age.

Before the first surfaced roads connecting the north with the south were built, the northern regency was more exposed to international influences than to southern influences. Bugis traders from Sulawesi frequented the northern port, Chinese and Muslim traders made Singaraja their home, and then there were the Dutch. Many of the buildings in Singaraja attest to the various international influences it has experienced through the centuries; and the Chinese Temple, mosques and Christian churches bear testimony to the diversity.

"Singaraja" means "lion king", and the huge winged lion statue at the intersection of Jl. Veteran and Jl. Ngurah Rai, built as a monument to Indonesian Independence, represents the heroic spirit of the people of Buleleng. The pentagonal plinth symbolises the *pancasila* (the five creeds of Indonesia), the lion's wings each have 17 feathers, the cob of corn he holds has eight leaves, and with the 45 grains of corn they represent August 17, 1945: the day of Indonesian Independence.

HOW TO GET THERE

By Public Bemo

A regular express bus departs from Ubung terminal in Denpasar, to Singaraja's Banyusari terminal in the west. The journey takes two hours, travels via Bedugul, and the fare is Rp2500. From Kereneng terminal in Denpasar, the bemo travels along the eastern coast road, via Gianyar, Klungkung and Amlapura, to Singaraja's eastern terminal, Kampung Tinggi. The journey takes five hours and costs Rp2500.

Bemos also run from the terminals in Klungkung and Amlapura and cost Rp2000.

Bemos to and from Gilimanuk cost Rp2100, and arrive and depart from the Banyusari terminal in Singaraja.

By Car

There are many ways to reach Singaraja from Denpasar, and the roads are sealed. The most direct route is 78km (48 miles) and takes about two to three hours, via Mengwi, Baturityi and Bedugul to Singaraja. Or, the eastern coast road passes

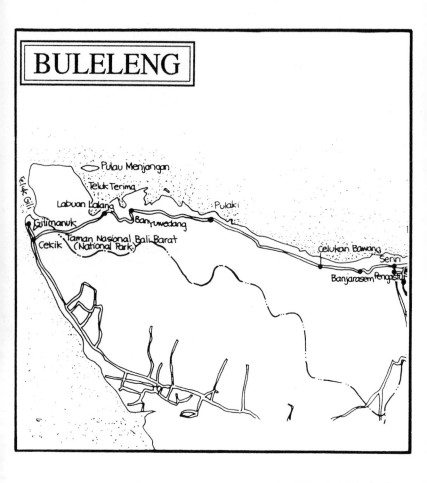

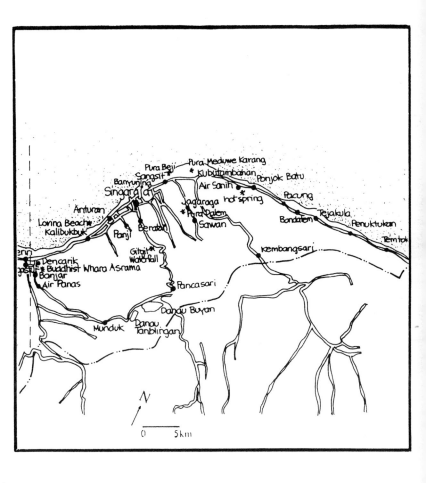

through Gianyar, Klungkung, Amlapura, Tirta Gangga, Kubu, then to Singaraja. This route takes about five hours but the views are stunning; Gunung Agung on one side, the sea on the other.

TOURIST INFORMATION

The Buleleng Government Tourism Office is located at Jl. Veteran 23, ph 61 141.

ACCOMMODATION

Few travellers stay in Singaraja, as Lovina is only 10km (6 miles) away and has many fine hotels with the accustomed comforts. Most of Singaraja's hotels are located on Jl. A. Yani, and are losmen-style accommodation. Anyway, if you really want to stay in Singaraja here are a few addresses.

Hotel Duta Karya, Jl. A. Yani, next to the Garuda office has simple rooms with fans — quite up-market compared with some. Room Rp10,000.

Hotel Gelasari, Jl. A. Yani 87, is better value for money.

LOCAL TRANSPORT

By Public Bemo

Singaraja has two bemo terminals: Kampung Tinggi on the eastern side (Jl. Surapati) and Banyusari on the western side (Jl. A. Yani). Bemos run frequently between these stations using the main roads, and dokars ply the back roads.

Bemos around the city cost Rp150, and a bemo to Lovina costs Rp400 (although "tourist fares" are popular).

By Car

Travelling around Singaraja by car is much easier than negotiating the streets of Denpasar. And finding a park is not impossible.

There are two petrol stations in Singaraja and one at Seririt.
Jl. A. Yani, near the Banyuasri bemo station.
Jl. Patih Jelantik Gingsir.
Jl. W. R. Surpratman (Kubujati/Penarukan), Seririt.

EATING OUT

Singaraja has many Chinese restaurants and a few serve Indonesian food. **Most of them are found along Jl. A. Yani.**
Gandi's. On Jl. A. Yani is famous for its Chinese food. Its menu is extensive and the prices are very reasonable. *Kartika's* next door, is also good.

The night markets have a huge range of warungs and fruit stalls set up in back lanes behind Jl. Gaja Mada.

ENTERTAINMENT

Unfortunately, there are no Balinese dance shows for visitors because all theatre performances are part of ceremonies, so finding this type of entertainment is purely chance. The tourist office does not supply information on any kinds of entertainment.

There are however, three cinemas:
Singaraja Theatre, Jl. Surapati, ph 21 391.
Wijaya Theatre, Jl. Pramuka 42, ph 41 627.
Bioskop Muda Ria, Jl. Ngurah Rai.

SHOPPING

Singaraja is not a good place to shop, however, general items are much cheaper than those found in the south, so stock up.

There are two art/antique shops worth a browse: Miranda's Jl. A. Yani; and Srikandi, Jl. Diponegoro 46.

MISCELLANEOUS

Medical Services

Rumah Sakit Umum (public hospital), Jl. Ngurah Rai, ph 41 046. Dr Kwari Dermawan, Jl. A. Yani 58.

Money Changers

A few hotels change money, but banks are the best bet. Generally banks do not give cash advances on the fantastic plastic, and in these parts, the plastic isn't so fantastic as few shops accept them.

Bank Negara Indonesia, Jl. Surapati, ph 41 340.

Bank Bumi Daya, Jl. Erlangga 14, ph 41 245.

Bank Dagang Negara, Jl. A. Yani, ph 41 344.

Bank Pembangunan Daerah, Jl. A. Yani 56, ph 21 245.

Bank Perniagaan Umum, Jl. Gajah Mada, ph 21 491.

Bank Rakyat Indonesia, Jl. Ngurah Rai 14, ph 41 245.

Bank Seri Partha, Jl. Ngurah Rai, ph 61 252.

Photo Developers

Fuji, Jl. A. Yani.

Reflex, Jl. Diponegoro.

Post Office

Jl. Gaja Mada 158.

Jl. Jenderal Sudirman 68.

Telephones

The telephone/telegraph offices are located at Jl. Letkol Wisnu 2, and Jl. Gaja Mada 154 (next to the post office).

SIGHTSEEING

Gedong Kirtya Library

On Jl. Veteran (next door to the Tourism Office), is a library that houses a collection of Balinese literature and religious texts all inscribed on palm leaves, known as *lontar*. Other manuscripts are etched onto metal plates *prasastis*, and are among the earliest written documents found on the island. Visitors are can observe scribes painstakingly translating the texts, or examine the manuscripts themselves.

The library is the only one of its kind in Indonesia and was built in 1928, during the colonial period.

Opening times are Sunday to Monday 7am-1pm; Friday 7-11am; and Saturday 7am-noon.

Puri Agung Sinar Nadi

Behind the library is a textile factory housed in the Puri Kawan or "Western Court" of the former palace of the King of Singaraja. Here visitors can watch women weaving *kain tenun* cloth on huge wooden looms. Beautiful sashes and *kain* (the female equivalent to the sarong) can be purchased at reasonable prices — remember one piece of cloth can take a month to weave! There is another weaving factory, Berdikari, on Jl. Dewi Sartika.

Buleleng Harbour

On the north coast lies the once busy harbour of Buleleng. When Singaraja was the capital of the island, the harbour was an important trade route. Since 1958, when Denpasar became the capital, a new port was established in Celukan, 40km (25 miles) west of Singaraja. Today, Buleleng harbour is little used. The monument that juts out over the sea is called Yudha Mandala Tama, and commemorates the death of a freedom fighter killed by machine-gun fire from a Dutch warship.

EAST OF SINGARAJA

Banyuning

Known for its pottery, this little village is situated a kilometre east of Singaraja. The village makes everything from urns and vases, to roof tiles; and all the pieces are unglazed as there are no kilns available.

Sangsit

Located 8km (5 miles) east of Singaraja, the village has one of the finest temples in the regency, the Pura Beji temple. Built in the 15th century, it is dedicated to the rice goddess, Dewi Sri, and is owned by the members of the local irrigation board, or *subak.* Standing in the middle of a rice field, this temple illustrates the distinctive filigree style of architecture found in Buleleng.

An ornately carved pink, sandstone gateway, flanked by serpents, and decorated with demons and frangipani, marks the entrance, and kind-looking statues bid welcome. Inside the temple, the shrines are intricately and masterfully carved.

Not far from Pura Beji, is the temple of the dead, Pura Dalem. The walls of the temple are engraved with reliefs depicting stories from Balinese mythology, and one particular story, *Bima*, relates the travels of the soul through heaven and hell, determined by *karma*.

Jagaraga

About 7km (4 miles) beyond the Pura Beji is the turn for Jagaraga. In 1849, trapped by Dutch forces, Djilantik's consort and her retinue walked into the enemy gunfire rather than submit to the foe. Today, the only visible sign of the Dutch presence is found in the Pura Dalem.

On the left, as one enters the village from the main road, is the Pura Dalem, a temple dominated by the spirit of Rangda the witch. But the highlight of the temple, is the carvings that feature caricatures of Westerners — more than likely the Dutch. In one, two rotund Dutchmen, in a chauffer-driven Model "T" Ford, are accosted by an armed bandit; and another presents an aerial dogfight between aeroplanes.

Sawan

Several kilometres inland from Jagaraga, Sawan is noted for its manufacture of Balinese *gamelan* instruments. The village also has its own bamboo orchestra, known as an *angklung*. Visitors are more than welcome to watch the gong-makers at work.

Kubutambahan

The village is 20km (12 miles) east of Singaraja, about a

kilometre past the Kintamani turn-off. The **Pura Meduwe Karang**, or "temple of the god of dry land" is a place of worship to ensure that crops such as corn, coffee and fruit prosper on unirrigated land. The temple is one of the largest in the regency and is built in the distinctive Buleleng style, although it is not as grand as the Pura Beji.

A stone staircase leads to the temple proper, a bare open courtyard which accommodates a huge pyramid-like plinth with two small pavilions (*bales*) where offerings are laid. More steps lead to the inner sanctum, which is dominated by a huge throne decorated with figures from the *Ramayana* intertwined with floral designs. Another pedestal has a carving of Siwa's consort, Durga, the merciless goddess of destruction. The most famous of the reliefs is of the Dutch painter, Nieuwenkamp, riding a bicycle with a lotus flower for the back wheel.

Air Sanih

Adjacent to the beach is the pretty landscaped swimming pool known as Air Sanih. The icy cold water is said to flow from a natural spring that originates at Lake Batur, and the clear pool is ideal for a swim, as is the pint-sized kiddies pool. Nearby, the manicured Botanic Gardens create a beautiful and serene place to spend the day. A warung and bungalows are available.

Ponjok Batu

On the coast, 7km (4 miles) east of Air Sanih is the village of Ponjok Batu. The temple, Pura Ponjok Batu, stands atop a hill offering spectacular views of the ocean and surrounding frangipani. Across the road is a small shrine of fenced rocks where the itinerant priest Nirartha is said to have rested, composing poetry inspired by the beauty of the panorama.

Sembiran

From Pacung, a steep meandering road, affording views of

terraces and plantations, leads travellers to Sembiran. This is the home of a group of pre-Majapahit "Bali Aga" or original Balinese. Sadly, the village is rather neglected, and the people, impoverished. Despite their isolation they are very hospitable.

About a kilometre before the village is the temple. Nestled on a hill, the temple has visible signs of Hindu influences, although the layout is pre-Hindu.

Tejakula Village

About 3km (2 miles) past the Sembiran turn-off is the village of Tejakula. The tiny village is home to a royal horse bath decorated with elaborate white arches and fed by intricately carved spouts. Nearby is a public swimming pool.

SOUTH OF SINGARAJA

Beratan Village

Located south of Singaraja (travel down Jl. Veteran and turn right, heading for Denpasar) is this village of silversmiths. Noted for their original style, sometimes referred to as the "Buleleng style", the silversmiths craft ornate jewellery and ceremonial pieces, which border on the rococo. The style is probably not to everyone's liking, but watching the silversmiths work is interesting.

Gitgit Waterfall

The dramatic waterfalls of Gitgit, 10km (6 miles) south of Singaraja, are just the thing for weary travellers. The road climbs steeply, affording picturesque views of lush hillocks, and the waterfall is located on a trail less than a kilometre from the main road. A pretty place: the large rock pool at the bottom, with clear, cool water is ideal for a refreshing dip, and an invigorating mist hangs in the air. But the area isn't as isolated as you might expect, and a warung and picnic area have been built by the base of the falls.

Pancasari Village and Bali Handara Country Club

About 13km (9 miles) south of Gitgit is the renowned Bali Handara Golf Club. Rated in the top 20 courses in the world, and the top five in Asia, the 18-hole golf course was designed by the former international Australian golfer, Peter Thompson according to international standards. Surrounded by luxuriant, tropical scenery and two lakes, the course must have one of the best views in the world. Green fees are US$60 for 18 holes, and a half-set of clubs can be hired for US$10.

The Country Club (catering to those with a fetish for hitting little while balls with long sticks into little holes) is a luxury hotel with full amenities including a sauna and fitness centre. Rooms from US$80-$300.

Panji

Located 10km (6 miles) south-west of Singaraja is the village noted for its unique "crow" dance, as well as its Independence monument. The Balinese who fought against the Dutch in 1848 made a pact to erect a monument, if they won. After Indonesian Independence, the Balinese planted two banyan trees, to represent the red and white of the new Indonesian flag; and the trees were planted 17 metres apart to signify the 17th, the day of independence. Later, in 1966, the Bhuwana Kertha Monument proper was erected. The monument is 17 metres high, with 45 spouts, and eight water lilies on the top of the column, all representing August 17, 1945. The plinth is in the shape of a pentagon and symbolises the five principles of Indon- esia, known as the *pancasila*.

LOVINA BEACH

Located 10km (6 miles) west of Singaraja is the tourist resort of Lovina, which actually includes the beaches of Anturan, Kalibukbuk, Lovina and Temukas. "Lovina" was supposedly coined in the 1960s by the last Raja of Buleleng, who felt that the love the people bore the land was reflected in the scenery. Since the late 1970s, restaurants and losmen have sprouted, and although tourism has increased, Lovina is very different from the south. An exquisite beach, the atmosphere is relaxed, and the pace, slow. The night-life focuses on eating, and with the plethora of seafood, that's not a bad thing (if you like fish). As yet, there are few hawkers, but they're sure to increase.

Although Kuta is famous for its sunsets, the vision of the glistening orb slowly sinking on this coastal strip, is at least comparable, some say better. **The still waters and shimmering black sands make Lovina twilights simply stunning**. As the sun descends the sky turns red, yellow, then orange — the sort of display one expects from trick photography. **The snorkelling is also especially good for beginners as the reef is close to the beach and the shallow water is placid.** On the morn, watch schools of *dolphins* frolicking close to the shore.

HOW TO GET THERE

By Public Bemo

In Singaraja, bemos travel during the daylight hours to Lovina, picking up along Jl. A. Yani. The fare is Rp400.

To reach Lovina from Denpasar, Karangasem or Gilimanuk you must change at Singaraja. For information on "How to get There", see the same in section on Singaraja.

By Car

Coming from the south or east, you have to drive through Singaraja to arrive at Lovina.
See the "How to get There" section.

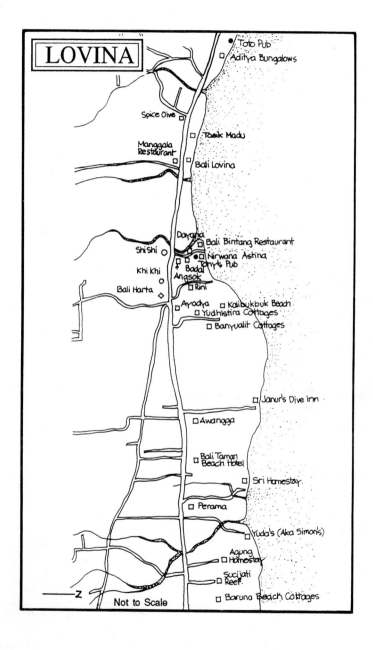

ACCOMMODATION

All rates, which should be used as a guide only, are based on one night and are in US$, generally including service charges. First class hotels really don't exist, but prices are much cheaper than in the south, and are usually negotiable in the low season.

Many losmen-style hotels are situated on the beach, and newer hotels are invariably set away from the beach. Again, they're much cheaper than in the south and it's best to shop around.

The telephone code is 0362.

Bali Lovina Beach Cottages, Kalibukbuk, ph 41 385. Set on the beach; the cottages are built around a pool. Room $45-$55, plus 15.5% tax and service charges and breakfast.

Bali Taman Beach Hotel, on the main road in Tukad Mungga. There are some airconditioned rooms. Room $40-$45, plus 15.5% tax and service charges.

Banyualit Cottages, Kalibukbuk, ph 41 889. About 50 metres from the beach, the service is excellent. Ask for an airconditioned room. The restaurant is good and specialises in seafood and Chinese meals. Room $30-$40 with airconditioning, includes service charges.

Baruna Beach Cottages, Lovina, ph 41 252. Right on the beach with its own pool. Ask for Agung or Batur rooms; room $35-55, includes service charges.

Kalibukbuk Beach Inn, at the end of Banyualit lane, ph 21 701. Ask for the newly refurbished rooms with airconditioning. Room $30.

Simon's Seaside Cottages (aka Yuda's), Antaran, ph 41 183. On the beach are four two-storey bungalows (ask for the second storey which has great views). Room $20-$25.

Suci Jati Reef, Antaran, ph 21 952. The bungalows are located between rice paddies and the beach. Room $10-$15.

Yudhistira Cottages, Banyualit Lane. Rooms have airconditioning and hot water. Room $20.

LOCAL TRANSPORT

Bemos are the easiest and cheapest form of transport. They travel along the coastal road and will generally pick up anywhere. Bemos east to Singaraja cost Rp400, and west to Banjar cost Rp600. The other alternative is to hitch-hike, which costs about the same as a bemo.

Cars and motorbikes can be hired from UD Simon in Kalibukbuk.

EATING OUT

Most hotels have a restaurant, and there are a few warungs in "Lovina".

Badai Restaurant, Kalibukbuk, has a varied menu tending towards Indonesian/Padang and the food is very tasty and cheap.

Banyualit Seafood Restaurant, in the hotel of the same name, has great seafood, and the Chinese cook varies the menu daily.

Hungarian Restaurant, Kalibukbuk, is a surprising find and the food is a pleasant surprise too.

Khi Khi, Kalibukbuk, has wonderful fresh lobster and crab which come with a selection of seven sauces. This is probably the busiest restaurant in town and it has a good atmosphere and a free dance performance.

Nirwana, Kalibukbuk, is a fun place and has some interesting Indonesian fare.

Tony's, Kalibukbuk, near the beach, has good food and is a fun place to spend an evening.

MISCELLANEOUS

Telephones are still a luxury, but international calls can be made from most hotels — they'll also change money. There are a couple of money changers in town, but the banks in Singaraja give slightly better rates.

For photo developing, go to Singaraja which has a number of one-hour developers. Generally, anything that can't be found or bought, can be procured in Singaraja, a ten-minute bemo ride from Kalibukbuk.

WATER ACTIVITIES

Scuba diving gear can be hired from *Spice Dive* in Lovina, or *Lovina Marine Resort*, Bali Lovina Beach Cottages.

Prahu can be rented from anywhere on the beach for about Rp4000 an hour, or from most hotels. As the water is not deep, swim out to the reef, but be sure to wear sneakers because the coral is sharp. It is advisable to swim early in the day as the water clouds, and with the black sand it is often difficult to determine the depth.

OUTLYING ATTRACTIONS

Singsing Falls

West of Lovina, about a kilometre along the main Seririt road, is the village of Labuanhaji and Singsing waterfall. Take a bemo from Lovina (Rp250) to the dirt road with the sign to Singsing Air Terjun. A short walk leads to the bottom pool, and another short climb to a second pool. Both are suitable for swimming, but only in the wet season. There is a third, secluded pool, which is a couple of hours' walk and requires a guide.

Banjar

The village of Banjar, about 5km (3 miles) west of Lovina, is an easy couple of hours walk. Alternatively, take a bemo (Rp200) along the main road, and from the turn-off on the left, rent a motorbike (with driver) for Rp400. The village market has a wonderful array of oddities, and the people are extremely friendly. From the intersection at Banjar, turn left to the village of Banjar Tegehe.

Buddhist Monastery

The monastery is worth a visit. Go to Banjar, and from the

main road, hire a motorbike to the monastery, or walk. The walk is long and steep, but the views are great. Actually, it's better to hire a bike up the hill and walk down, either back-tracking through Banjar, or follow the monastery road through Banjar Tegehe and Dencarik back to the main road. Dencarik is quite isolated and as few Westerners pass by, the kids love to stop and chat. Remember, if you're intending to walk, wear a hat and carry water!

The Brahma Vihara Asrama opened in 1970, and is the only Buddhist monastery on the island (there are Buddhist temples, but only one monastery). It was ruined in the earthquake of 1976, but is now fully restored. The complex is perched on a huge hill that affords views back to the coast, and across luscious plantations. Walk up the stairs to the small courtyard: immediately in front is the temple, to the right, the monastery, and to the left, an impressive bell tower (the bell hails from Thailand). Indeed this is a serenely beautiful sanctuary. The Dalai Lama visited in 1982, and in April and September, the monastery is closed as pilgrims from everywhere visit the monastery to pray.

The temple has a splendid gilt altar with intricate Buddhist motifs, and it is one of the most impressive and stirring sights on the island. But before entering, remove your shoes and speak only in hushed tones.

Air Panas

An hour's walk from the monastery are the hot springs of Banjar; or drive right up to the pools on the new sealed road. In 1985, the muddy waters were channelled into three public bathing pools, and the gardens were landscaped. The springs are sulphurous, but at 38C (100F), they are no less exhilarating.

Admission is Rp300.

Seririt

Located 22km (14 miles) from Singaraja, the once bustling trade capital of Buleleng is now a sleepy little town.

Devastated by the earthquake of 1976, it has been subsequently rebuilt.

From here, the road meanders inland, and hills and plantations dominate the scenery.

Celukan Bawang

About 16km (10 miles) from Seririt is the new trade port of Buleleng. This protected harbour was chosen as the new port because the old harbour at Singaraja was exposed to the elements and consequently dangerous.

Pulaki

Further west, is the village of Pulaki, about 53km (33 miles) from Singaraja, and the temple, Pura Agung Pulaki, is 2km (1 mile) from the main road. The large and striking temple, built between a sheer cliff and the lapping shore, is home to a band of rapacious monkeys. Take care with all belongings, there's no need to feed them as they scavenge the fruit and vegetables that fall from passing trucks.

It is said the temple is associated with the Javanese priest, Nirartha, who bestowed immortality on the inhabitants of the local village. These disembodied souls, called *gamang*, often visit the villagers who make offerings to placate them.

From Pulaki, there are more hot springs 4km (2.5 miles) down the road at Pemuteran, outside of the temple.

WEST BALI NATIONAL PARK

An hour's drive from Lovina is the Taman Nasional Bali Barat, the West Bali National Park. If not with an organised tour, it's a 15-minute drive to the guard-post (PPA) at Teluk Terima. Visitors must purchase a permit (Rp500) and a guide (Rp5000) is mandatory by law. The best source of information is found at the headquarters which are located at Cekik, 2km (1 mile) south of Gilimanuk (about as west as you can get). A government office, it's open during the week until 2pm, and closes at 11am on Fridays and noon on Saturdays. The staff are very helpful and enthusiastic, and there's even a small library and exhibition.

The national park has 76,312 ha of untouched flora and fauna, and whereas most of Bali seems to be terraced, or at least cultivated, western Bali is a natural wonderland. Although many visitors arrive from the Buleleng entrance, most of the park is actually located in the regency of Jembrana. The land was originally declared a national park by the Indonesian Forestry Service (Direktorat Perlindungan dan Pengawetan Alam) with the intention of preserving and conserving the wilderness.

This is the natural habitat of the rare *Jalak Bali* or "Bali Starling" (*Leucopsar rothschildi*). This beautiful coloured bird is found nowhere else in the world, and in fact, only a hundred or so remain. The starling is a brilliant white with black tail feathers, but its distinguishing features are the cobalt blue patches around its eyes. The wild Javan buffalo (*Bos javanicus*) is another rare species, with estimates of 30 individuals. Other wildlife include wild pigs, barking deer, leaf monkeys, and unique green fowl. The park is simply teeming with wildlife.

Banyuwedang

On the outskirts of the national park are the oft-visited springs of Banyuwedang. These glorious springs, according to local lore, have curative powers, and people come from miles around to splash in the salutary waters.

Pulau Menjangan

From the park's Buleleng entrance, it's a 15-minute drive to Teluk Terima where small motorised boats can be hired for the 30-minute crossing to Pulau Menjangan. This haven, also known as Deer Island, is the home of the Java Deer. There are no warungs, no bemos, few people — an idyllic sanctuary. Remember to take a packed lunch.

More enchanting than the deer, are the beautiful, psychedelic reefs. **The fish and coral, as well as the mild** currents, make this the ultimate place to dive in Bali.

Most scuba diving centres organise tours to Pulau Menjangan, but day tours from the south leave little time to explore the waters. **There are no rental places in the park, so it is advisable to organise tours from Lovina or Singaraja.**

NOTES

JEMBRANA

Jembrana would probably be ignored by travellers if it were not for the ferry terminal at Gilimanuk. Little of its mountainous jungle has been explored and myths of the regency's strange inhabitants abound. Once known as Jimbar Wana, the "Great Forest", most of Jembrana lies in the Bali Barat National Park. Bali's wild, wild west, it was once the hunting ground of the extinct Bali tiger. Today, the wilderness teems with wild pigs, deer, monkeys, fowl, and Bali's rare starling. The regency is sparsely populated owing to the impenetrable jungle, low rainfall and isolation, so most of the people who live there are found on the coast, eking out a living from the sea. Yet in recent years, small rice plantations have appeared and the population is realising the potential of clove farming.

In the 17th century, a Bugis prince, from what is now known as Sulawesi, installed himself as Raja of Jembrana. Later, in the 19th century, the Raja of Karangasem invaded and colonised the region. Then came the Dutch, who took control in 1847.

Negara is the capital of Jembrana, and as in the village of Gilimanuk, Hinduism has yielded to Islam. Owing to the regency's proximity to Java, Jembrana has the biggest Muslim and Christian communities on the island. Political refugees have sought sanctuary in the wilds of Jembrana.

FROM THE SOUTH TO NEGARA

Driving from the south through Tabanan, the road eventually ends at the intersection at Antosari. The road north leads past rice terraces to Pupuan, then Seririt, then hugs the north coast to Singaraja. The road south stretches past Soka and follows

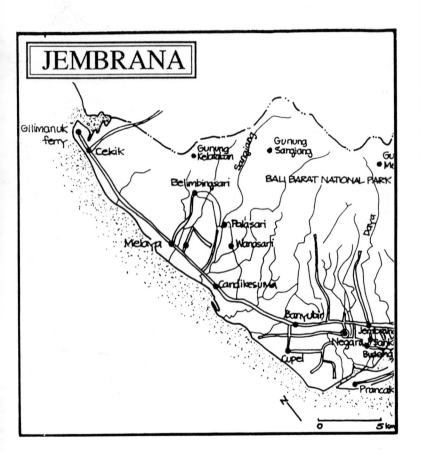

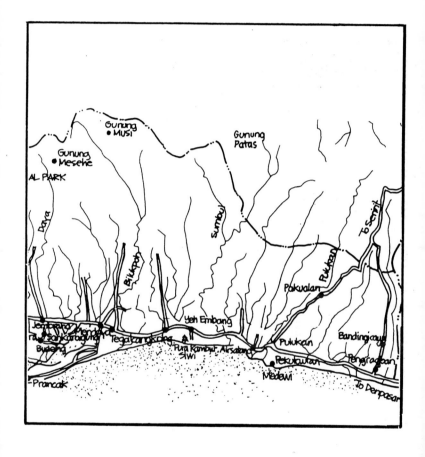

the south coast to Mendaya, then inland to Negara, finally arriving at Gilimanuk — not before some wonderful views across to Java.

The town of Pekutantan (20km (12 miles) east of Negara) is the last place to turn north for Singaraja. The road west eventually leads to Gilimanuk.

> West of Pekutantan, on the left from Denpasar, is the entrance to Medewi Beach. Black sands, hammering waves and simple losmen, not to mention the solitude, make this a great surfing spot.

Further west, near Yeh Buah, a small road leads down to the sea and the temple of Rambut Siwi. Perched high on a cliff, the little temple is a memorial to the much-loved priest, Nirartha. He is said to have cured the village of a plague and presented a lock of his hair to the people to protect them from further misfortune. Hence, the name, Rambut Siwi, "Siwa's hair".

NEGARA

The capital of the regency, Negara possesses a few government offices, a couple of losmen and a few small warungs. To a visitor it seems like a town in slumber. That is, until September, after the rice is harvested, when Negara is enlivened with spectacular bull races. The owners are extremely proud of their beasts and pamper them, sparing them the strenuous work of beasts of burden. Before the race, the decorated bulls are paraded before the spectators, then stripped in readiness for the race. Yoked in pairs, the bulls pull a chariot and jockey, and although the winner should cross the line first, the judges are fickle when it comes to strength, style and sartorial splendour. Of course, punters bet frantically, and besides the obvious prestige of winning, the bull is sure to make his owner a little richer.

A couple of kilometres east of Negara is **Sankaragung**. The village has a new museum devoted to the *gamelan*, and the proprietor, Ketut Suwentra, a musician, dancer and composer, is happy to show visitors around. There is no admission fee, but donations are appreciated.

Negara is 95km (59 miles) from Denpasar, and bemos depart from Tabanan (Rp900) or from Denpasar's Ubung terminal (Rp1500).

PALASARI AND BELIMGINGSARI

Many of the people living in these villages are Christian migrants from the overpopulated areas of eastern and southern Bali. The government granted them uncultivated land in the hope of developing the area, and the program was such a success that the villages were hailed as models for migration. The biggest Catholic church in eastern Indonesia is located in Palasari, and there are other denominations as well. But this is Bali and many of the churches are adorned with typical Balinese motifs, featuring biblical characters rather than those from the Hindu epics.

BALI BARAT NATIONAL PARK

For information on Bali's national park, see the section on Buleleng. Most people enter the park from the northern entrances, which are located in that regency.

GILIMANUK

Gilimanuk, on the westernmost tip of Bali, is the village where east meets west. Most of the domestic tourists enter and leave Bali via this port, as do imports and exports. This is not a tourist town, merely a place to embark or disembark, depending on your destination. Mind you, Muslims chanting in the local mosque is a nice contrast to the tones of the *gamelan* ringing from the local banjar.

In Singaraja, bemos leave the Banyuasri terminal (Rp1000) for Gilimanuk; and from Denpasar, bemos depart from the Ubung terminal (Rp2200) for the two-hour journey. Gilimanuk is 128km (80 miles) from Denpasar via Tabanan; and 85km (53 miles) from Singaraja, via Seririt and the National Park.

The Ferry

Despite the fact that the strait separating Bali from Java is less than 3km and is only 60m deep, the waters can be treacherous. The crossing takes 25 minutes, and both private and government ferries ply the route, departing at 15 to 20 minute intervals.

For passengers, the ferry prices range from Rp400 for the deck, to Rp1200 for first class; and stowage for motorbikes cost Rp1000; cars Rp7000.

The ferry docks in Java at Ketapang and buses leave from there to Surabaya.

NOTES

TABANAN

The regency of Tabanan stretches from the south-west coast all the way to the slopes of Gunung Batukau. The second-highest mountain in Bali, it is seldom spoken of, but Batukau dominates inland views, and has a beautiful ancestral shrine, Pura Luhur. Most visitors only venture to Tabanan to witness the splendour of sunset at Tanah Lot; or to spend a night in the mystical mountains of Bedugul, on the way to Lovina. **Tabanan has one of the highest yields of rice in Indonesia.** On the southern plains, rice is cultivated alternately with nitrogen-rich soybeans to revitalise the soil, and in the mountains, vegetables and flowers are grown. Some of the most stunning landscape is seen when driving from Denpasar through Bedugul to the north.

History

In the 11th century, Tabanan was controlled by the Javanese king, Erlangga, and was invaded in the 14th century by Gaja Mada, the prime minister of the Majapahit empire. Tabanan's renaissance occurred during the 17th century with the establishment of the palace at Tabanan. But the regency was constantly at battle with the old kingdom of Mengwi, and, aided by the princes of Badung, Mengwi was overthrown, and its land split between the two regencies.

In the 20th century, the Dutch, who already controlled the north, vanquished Tabanan and exiled those of the court who had not suicided, to Lombok. The absence of an agreement between the Dutch and the royalty, lead the Dutch to divide the land and redistribute it through the banjar — the bane of the royalty was to be the boon of the peasants. Since that time, the people have toiled to create a rich rice area.

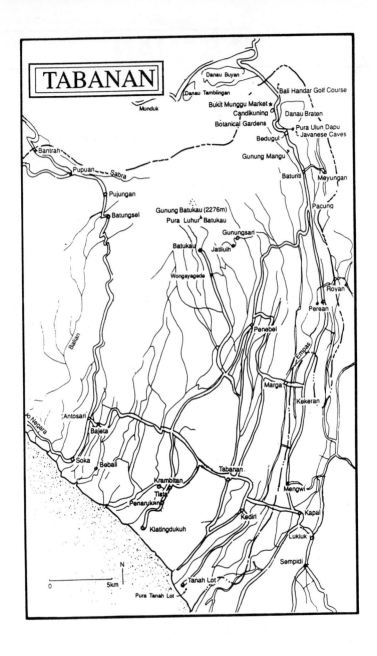

TABANAN TOWN

On the much-travelled road from Denpasar, not far from the Badung border, is the town of Tabanan. The capital of the regency, Tabanan is a commercial centre which few tourists deem worth seeing — a shame really, because the area is rich in tradition. The palace, Puri Tabanan, attests to the splendour of the once prosperous royalty.

Bali's most famous dancer, the late I Ketut Marya, or Mario, studied dance at the Puri Kaleran palace. He developed the frenetic *kebyar duduk* or sitting dance, where the performer dances in a crouched position while flirting with the accompanying drummer. He was also known for his *gandrung* (transvestite) dance performances. The Gedong Marya Theatre was established in 1974 as a memorial to the revered dancer and teacher.

Tabanan boasts an excellent *gamelan*, whose descendants created the bamboo *tingklik* orchestra. It's a pity there are no regular performances.

A kilometre east of Tabanan, in Sanggulan village, is the Subak Museum. *Subak* are the rice-growing co-operatives found all over Bali, and the museum houses an historical perspective on the formation and evolution of communal rice farming. There are a few small losmen and warungs located in the town, but this really is not a good place to stay overnight.

HOW TO GET THERE

By Bemo

Bemos depart from Denpasar's Ubung terminal and cost Rp700.

By Car

Tabanan is located 21km (13 miles) from Denpasar. By car,

take the main road north-west from Denpasar passing through the villages of Lukluk and Kapal.

OUTLYING ATTRACTIONS

Marga Village

About 15km (9 miles) north-east of Tabanan is the village of Marga. Here lies a national shrine to I Gusti Ngurah Rai, who in 1946, lead the Tabanan forces against the Dutch in a modern-day *puputan*. The shrine houses a stone tower with a carved replica of his refusal to capitulate, and 94 pedestals are monuments to his fellow martyrs. The hero's name is also honoured by the international airport.

Krambitan Village

West of Tabanan, 12km (7 miles) away, is the village known for its *tektekan* performance. Not so much a dance as an exorcism, it involves a procession of marching men adorned with wooden cow bells and drums. In times past, the exorcism occurred during times of disaster; now the performance is incorporated into the island's annual day of exorcism, *Nyepi*. Two palaces built by the Tabanan royal family are located here, and both offer rooms for rent. The old palace, Puri Krambitan (owned by the twin grandsons of the late king), has an ornate concert hall decorated with Chinese porcelain tiles. The second palace, Puri Anyar, holds performances of the Calon Arang trance dance which features Rangda the witch.

Yeh Panas

The springs, regarded as sacred by the locals, are located 12km (7 miles) north of Tabanan on the way to Pura Luhur on the slopes of Gunung Batukau. The hot sulphurous springs were used by the Japanese stationed in Tabanan during the war.

TANAH LOT

The regency's main attraction is the temple at Tanah Lot. One of the six *sad kahyangan* temples, it is visited by more tourists than any other sight in Bali. Definitely overrated, the temple simply doesn't have the atmosphere, nor the beauty, of Ulu Watu. Built on a diminutive rocky island, it's a short walk from the shore and accessible only during low tide. Not that that matters. The temple is locked and tourists are not permitted in. Most people only visit to take photographs, and by the way, the best shots are taken from the headland on the left when facing the temple.

The priest, Nirartha, advised the local village to build a temple. He was, not surprisingly, enamoured of the south coast. Now, bus loads of tourists land at Tanah Lot just before sunset, cameras poised for the breath-taking shot of the petite pagodas as they form a silhouette against the sky. Don't visit on an overcast day, for the sunset will be shrouded in clouds.

Poisonous black snakes live amongst the rocks and a monstrous, "holy" snake, is said to guard the temple.

> Tanah Lot can actually be reached by following the beach from Kuta, but only at low tide and be prepared to get drenched. Most hotels in Kuta and Sanur provide **tours** to Tanah Lot, but they **are expensive when compared to a bemo ride.**

Parking costs Rp500 and admission to the site is Rp500. Temple sashes must be worn.

Bemos depart from Denpasar's Ubung terminal to Kediri (Rp700), then change for Tanah Lot (Rp300). If returning by bemo, don't linger after sunset or you'll miss out.

By car from Denpasar, take the road which eventually leads to Tabanan and turn left at the stoplight at Kediri which leads right down to the carpark at Tanah Lot.

GUNUNG BATUKAU

Called the "coconut-shell mountain", this extinct volcano is the biggest mountain in the western part of the chain that severs north Bali from the south. The volcano is 2275m (7464ft) high and is carpeted with dense rainforest. On its slopes lies Pura Luhur, one of Bali's six national temples belonging to the *sad kahyangan* group. Guides can be hired if you want help to climb the mountain, as the ascent can be very dangerous.

Pura Luhur is a holy ancestral temple built in deference to the gods of the mountains and lakes. The regency of Tabanan is not represented in the complex at Besakih, because the regency claims Pura Luhur as its state temple. At the time of the *Galungan* festival, thousands make the pilgrimage to this simple, moss-laden temple. Surrounded by dense forests, the small complex is located in a landscaped clearing. Thatched-roof *meru* towers abound, the highest being the seven-tiered pagoda associated with Maha Dewa, the deity of Batukau. East of the temple are steps leading to a cement pool complete with tiny island — a miniature lake.

BEDUGUL

Once upon a time, tourists seeking the quietude of the mountains fled to Ubud. Thankfully, most of them hadn't heard of Bedugul and environs. In fact, it's still a well-kept secret. Bedugul is a serene little village huddling on the shores of Lake Bratan in the crater of the long-extinct volcano, Gunung Catur (2096m - 6877ft). As far from the tropical coastal landscape as is possible, **Bedugul** and its sister village, **Candikuning,** are true mountain retreats. By early afternoon, the still lake and surrounding mountains are often shrouded in thick, white clouds, creating a mystical ambience. The cool, crisp, exhilarating mountain air makes the south seem like a carcinogenic dustbin. It's so cool, kids play football (well, at least in the dry season).

Make sure you pack a jumper because it gets quite cold at night.

The cool clime, high rainfall, and rich volcanic soils make Bedugul and vicinity a fertile area producing most of the flowers found on Bali. **The market, Bukit Mangsu, has a wondrous array of flowers, as well as bargain fruit and vegetables.**

For those who enjoy watersports, there's water skiing, jet skiing, parasailing, or simply paddle a canoe across Lake Bratan. The Bedugul Hotel can arrange all water sports, but for canoe hire, check out the boys near the Ashram Hotel. For landlubbers, there are beautiful scenic walks up Gunung Catur, or explore the Botanic Gardens.

Not far from Bedugul is the famous Bali Handara Country Club and world-class golf course. For more information, see the section on Buleleng (the regency in which the course is located).

HOW TO GET THERE

By Bemo

Bemos depart from Denpasar's Ubung terminal for Bedugul and Candikuning, and cost Rp1000. The trip takes about an hour and a half.

By Car

Bedugul is 48km (30 miles) from Denpasar and 30km (19 miles) from Singaraja. The road from Denpasar to Bedugul eventually ends at Singaraja. The views are spectacular, especially before Bedugul, where high in the mountains, the landscape is filled with beautiful hillocks, majestic mountains and glassy lakes. Although the road is much travelled, the animals don't seem to remember this and chickens, dogs, cattle, even monkeys, amble onto the road with little thought of their impending peril. Drive only during the daylight hours and take care on the hairpin turns.

ACCOMMODATION

Prices based on one night's accommodation are in US$, and should be used as a guide only.

Pacung, Baturiti, ph (0361) 226 531. Recently opened, this is the most luxurious hotel in the area. It is set amidst hillocks and has superb views. All rooms have hot water, and there's even a swimming pool. Room US$60.

Bedugul Hotel, Bedugul, ph (0361) 226 593. The hotel has 16 luxury bungalows and 15 standard rooms overlooking Lake Bratan, and all rooms have hot water. The hotel also has water skiing, jet skiing, parasailing and rowing facilities. Room standard US$12, luxury US$20-$30 (tax & service charges not included).

Ashram Hotel, Candikuning. Right on the lake, the hotel has rooms overlooking the lake, and every room has hot water — a must. A real bargain! Room US$15.

Bukit Mungsu Indah, Baturiti, ph Baturiti 22. Cosy rooms with fireplaces (some overlooking the Botanic Gardens), make this a nice place to stay. Room US$20-$30.

There are many small losmen in Bedugul village, near the botanic gardens. Don't be reluctant to bargain.

LOCAL TRANSPORT

Bemos operate between Bedugul and Candikuning and cost Rp300, but it's only a refreshing 20-minute walk between villages.

EATING OUT

There are only a few warungs in Bedugul and Candikuning,

but all the hotels listed above have restaurants.

Perama Tea House, Candikuning. A small restaurant near Ulu Danu Temple, which has very pretty views of the lake and manicured gardens. Reasonably priced, standard tourist Indonesian fare.

Kamandalu Restaurant, Bali Handara Country Club. If you're mobile this is a nice place to eat dinner.

TOURIST ATTRACTIONS

Botanical Gardens

Half a kilometre from the lake (towards Denpasar) is the Kebun Raya Eka Karya Bali, or botanical gardens. Formerly an orchid plantation, the gardens were declared a national park in 1959 to enable the study of the flora of eastern Indonesia. The gardens cover 129.2 ha (52 acres) of wooded parkland and offer over 600 species of trees, many of which are labelled.

There are beautiful walks amongst flowers and trees, and there is an information centre near the entrance. Guides can be hired from the Bedugul Hotel.

The park is open from 8am until 4.30pm, and admission is Rp500.

Pura Ulun Danu Bratan

On the shores of Lake Bratan, Candikuning, is Pura Ulun Danu, dedicated to the goddess of the lake, Dewi Danu. Much revered for her powers over fertility, she also favours the people with the vital waters of the lake. Built right on the shores of Lake Bratan, two courtyards, one with an 11-tiered pagoda, are surrounded by water. When the clouds descend, obscuring much of the mountains, the temple has an ethereal atmosphere — much more dramatic than other oft-visited temples. The main complex on the shore, Pura Teratai Bang, is a temple of "origin" and is dedicated to Brahma. You may notice the monumental Buddhist stupa, a reminder of the co-existence of Buddhism and Hinduism.

Admission is Rp500 and remember to wear a sash. Water-proof shoes are a must, because the complex is muddy all year round.

Japanese Caves

Across the lake from Candikuning (adjacent to the Bedugul Hotel) are the Japanese caves. These caves were excavated by Indonesian POWs during the Second World War, who were shot when they completed their task. The caves are accessible by canoe or from the trail that wanders up the rim of Gunung Catur. Canoes can be hired from Candikuning or Bedugul for Rp10,000 an hour. Caves are caves are caves, one might say, but these are particularly eerie.

Hikes

The walk up Gunung Mangu, on the south-eastern side of Lake Bratan is invigorating. A guide is essential and can be hired from the Bedugul Hotel, Ashram Hotel or at the markets. Only for the fit, the ascent takes over two hours, but it's quicker going down. The last half an hour of the climb involves dragging oneself with the aid of flora through steep, muddy tracts, and can be quite dangerous.

Don't even consider this climb in the wet season. On the rim of the crater is an ancient temple, Pura Pucak, built by the first Raja of Mengwi. The temple is simple, but the view is worth it.

Another hike begins at the northern end of the Botanical Gardens, and ventures along a well-marked path across the southern slopes of Gunung Tapak. The 8km (5 miles) walk leads to the village of Pancasari in the regency of Buleleng. This easy walk does not require a guide.

NOTES

GLOSSARY

aben cremation or the cremation ceremony.

adat traditional law or custom; unwritten code of conduct governing behaviour, inheritance, ownership of land, rituals of birth, marriage and death, rice cultivation, courtship etc. *Adat* is the law of the land and the oldest and most respected law at that.

Agama Bali Balinese Hindu religion otherwise known as Tirta Agama, Religion of the Holy Water.

agung great, big.

air panas literally, hot springs.

aling aling a wall behind the entrance gate to a family compound or temple which prevents demons from entering - it seems demons have problems negotiating corners.

alun alun the main town square, usually an expanse of lawn for sporting events and festivals etc.

angklung an ensemble of bamboo instruments.

anjing a dog, usually a pet; see *cecing*.

arak distilled palm or rice brandy.

Arjuna one of the five Pandawa brothers in the *Mahabharata*.

babi guling spit-roasted suckling pig.

bade funeral tower.

bale open-air pavilion, supported by posts.

bale agung a large pavilion where the village elders gather.

bale banjar village clubhouse where the banjar meets, and the site of community events; also where the *gamelan* orchestra rehearses.

Bali Aga indigenous, pre-Hindu inhabitants who resisted the cultural, social and political influences of the Majapahit Empire.

balian healer or traditional leader.

banjar village council consisting of married men who organise local affairs.

banten offerings to the gods.

banteng wild cattle of Indonesia.

banyan a sacred tree for the Balinese, usually a fig, with tangled roots which sprawl for metres around the tree. Also the tree under which Buddha found enlightenment. The *banyan* is supposedly eternal, feeding itself from the seeds, which drop on the ground. Temples and houses are often built near the site of a *banyan* tree.

bapak mister, father; the polite form of address to an older man.

baris warrior dance.

barong based on the 10th century Javanese king, Erlangga. Although a monstrous-looking creature, the Barong is a goodie who struggles against the evil witch Rangda (Erlangga's mother Mahendratta), in the *calon arang* myth. The barong is also a dance which features these characters.

Bedulu the last ruler of the Pejeng dynasty, defeated by the Majapahit minister, Gaja Mada in 1343AD.

Beh! an exclamation of surprise.

bemo a privately owned truck used for public transport.

betel slightly narcotic nut of *areca* palm, chewed with the leaf of the *sirih* vine and lime paste. *Pedanda* often chew the concoction, which leaves a red stain around the mouth.

betutu bebek roast duck.

Bima a warrior from the *Mahabharata* epic. One of the five Pandawa brothers, and a symbol of invincibility.

Boma deity of the earth.

Brahma four-headed Hindu god of creation, leader of the Hindu trinity.

Brahman the highest caste in Bali - the priestly caste.

brem black-rice wine.

Bupati head of one of the eight regencies on Bali.

Calon Arang mythical struggle between Mahendratta (the witch, Rangda), the Queen of Udayana, and her son Erlangga (the Barong), now depicted in the Barong dance.

candi bentar split gate entrance to temples.

cecing a mangy, homeless dog, despised by all.

cili palm-leaf effigy of the rice goddess, Dewi Sri.

colt a minibus for hire.

dalang shadow-puppet master.

danau lake.

dedari angels.

desa a village in the countryside.

dewa a god or honoured ancestor.

Dewa Agung title of utmost ruler of Bali.

dewi a goddess or divinity.

Dewi Danau goddess of the lake.

Dewi Sri goddess of rice and fertility.

pony-drawn cart.
a consort of Siwa; goddess of death destruction.

a Desa Rudra a ceremony held every undred years at the "mother temple" to purify the entire island. Last performed in 1979.
endek woven cloth.

Gaja Mada a prime minister of the Javanese Majapahit Empire who conquered Bali in 1343AD.
Galungan the most important yearly festival on Bali, lasting ten days, to mark the new year of the "oton" calender and is a celebration of creation.
gambuh ancient form of dance from which most dances are derived; rarely performed.
gamelan a generic term for any Balinese orchestra using bronze or wooden percussion instruments.
Ganesha the fat-bellied son of Siwa; god of homes and learning.
gang alley.
Garuda a mythical bird, like a cross between an eagle and a roc. Siwa's mount. Also the emblem of the Indonesian Republic and name of the international airline.
geko chameleon-like lizard found in Balinese homes, restaurants, known for the "hiccupping" noises it makes.
gedong large building, pavilion or museum.
Gelgel a Balinese kingdom during the 15th, 16th and 17th centuries.
geringsing a rare cloth in which both the weft and the warp are tie-dyed before weaving. Found only in the *Bali Aga* village of Tenganan.
gunung mountain.
guru teacher.

halus refined, elegant and noble behaviours and cultural traits.
Hanuman the white monkey king who upholds good in the *Ramayana* epic.

ibu mother, also a term of deference for older women.
ikat a tie-dye technique applied to either the warp or weft where the threads are tightly bound so as not to absorb the dye. The process is repeated to add different colours and patterns.
Indra god of the rain and thunder.

jaba outside; used to describe the *Sudra* caste of people outside of the *Triwangsa*, the three high castes.
jaja Balinese rice cakes.
jalan street.
jam karet rubber time (a literal translation). Reason for "elasticity" in

timetables, etc.
jeroan inner temple sanctuary.
joged the flirting dance, originated in Buleleng.
jukung small outrigger canoe.

Kabupaten one of the eight administrative districts based on the realms of the rajas.
kain length of fabric tied around the waist, falling to the ankles - similar to a sarong.
kain poleng black and white chequered cloth often tied around statues. The cloth admits both lightness and darkness, acknowledging both good and evil.
kaja north; towards Gunung Agung which is sacred, heavenly and positive - a pole of the axis upon which most buildings are constructed.
kala evil; also the son of Siwa and the god of malice.
kangin east; direction of the rising sun.
kantor office.
karma Hindu belief that destiny is determined by actions in this life and previous lives.
kasar a term for crude, impolite, coarse or inelegant behaviour.
kauh west; direction of the setting sun.
Kawi literary language known as Old Javanese, now only used in Balinese theatre.
kebaya ceremonial blouse. Traditionally, Balinese women were bare-breasted, but after the Dutch invasions women started to wear the Malay *kebaya*.
kecak the monkey dance, an excerpt from the *Ramayana* epic. A choral performance characterised by the "chukka, chukka" of monkeys.
kelod south; towards the sea, which is evil, negative and unlucky - opposite to the *kaja* pole.
kretek Indonesian clove cigarette, very sweet and numbing (due to the anaesthetic properties of the cloves).
kris a double-edged ceremonial dagger.
Krishna a manifestation of Wisnu, and a popular god in his own right.
kulkul a drum, often perched in a *banyan* tree which warns of danger, heralds or calls.
Kuningan the last day of the ten day *Galungan* ceremony, usually for ancestral deities.

lawar a ceremonial food concocted of shredded vegetables and meats.
legong graceful dance performed by young girls.
leyak a roaming, mischievous spirit.
lingga a phallic image and the symbol of Siwa.
lontar palm-leaf books.

losmen a small homestay or guesthouse available for rent and much cheaper than hotels.

Mahabharata an Indian Hindu epic poem describing the origins of the Hindu gods. The climax recounts the legendary battle between the Pandawa brothers, the "goodies" and their cousins, the Korawas, the "baddies". The poem was translated into *Kawi* in the Middle Ages, and is featured in literature, art and dance.

Majapahit great Hindu Empire established in Java, later moving to Bali in the 14th century. The kingdom had a profound effect on the culture, art and political organisation of Bali.

mandi a tub for bathing; to bathe.

meru tiered shrine.

negara a state, realm, capital, court, town or village.

Nirartha, Danghyang a Javanese priest who crossed to Bali after the fall of the Majapahit Empire. He acquired great fame through his teachings and gathered many disciples. He is associated with the temples at Ulu Watu and Tanah Lot, to name two.

nusa island.

Nyepi a day of silence to confuse evil spirits.

odalan temple anniversary festival.

oton a Balinese year of 210 days.

padi rice field.

padmasana high lotus throne used by the gods when they descend from heaven, often found in the inner sanctum of a temple.

Pancasila "The Five Principles"; a political philosophy introduced by Sukarno before Indonesian Independence as a basis for a constitution. Most Balinese have to recite the five creeds before they can be employed in any government office. And all of them will admit they believe in the creeds, especially the belief in one god. But in reality, the *pancasila* (for the Balinese anyway), is a foreign philosophy imposed by a Muslim government.

pantai beach.

paras soft volcanic stone used for statues.

pedanda Brahman priest.

pemangku non-Brahman temple curator or priest.

pendet welcoming procession.

penjor tall bamboo poles adorned with bamboo decorations that arch over streets during Galungan.

potong gigit tooth-filing ceremony.

prahu small wooden sailing boat or outrigger.

puputan literally, "the end"; a ritualised fight to the death or a mass suicide charge.

pura temple.

puri palace.

Ramayana an Indian epic which tells of the struggles between the hero Rama (Wisnu reincarnated) and the evil King Rawana, who abducts Rama's consort.

Rangda witch who struggles for supremacy against the Barong in the *Calon Arang* myth. She is based on Udayana's queen, Mahendratta, who is said to have practised black magic. As Rangda the witch, she is pitted against the Barong, Mahendratta's son Erlangga.

regency one of eight administrative districts on Bali based on the old kingdoms of the rajas. Also known as *Kabupaten*.

rijstaffel literally, "rice table" in Dutch. A smorgasbord of over forty Indonesian rice dishes, but the presentation is Dutch.

sad kahyangan state temples dedicated to the island, including Pura Besakih, Pura Uluwatu, Pura Tanah Lot, Pura Goa Lawah, Pura Batukau, Pura Pusering Jagat.

Sanghyang Widhi the Hindu Godhead; the omnipotent Hindu god. All deities, including Wisnu, Brahma and Siwa are manifestations of the cosmic force of Sanghyang Widhi. Well, that's according to intellectual Hindus intent on reconciling the *pancasila* with Hinduism.

Saraswati goddess of learning, literature and wisdom, and wife of Brahma.

Satrya the second-highest of the Hindu Bali caste, the warrior and ruling class.

sawah rice field.

sebel ritually unclean.

sirih a leaf of a species of pepper which is chewed by older Indonesians; the teeth and lips become rust-stained.

Siwa one of the Hindu trinity (Shiva for Indian Hindus). He is the Destroyer of the World, and is probably the most venerated because of his destructive powers. Siwa's emblem is the *lingga* or phallus.

subak village irrigation co-operative which oversees cultivation, irrigation and farming disputes.

suci holy, ritually clean.

Sudra those people outside of the Triwangsa caste system, which is about 90% of the population; Sudra is rarely used, most people refer to Sudra as *jaba*.

Surya the sun or the sun god.

suttee the rite of self-immolation by a widow at her husband's cremation; outlawed by the Dutch in the 19th century.

swastika the wheel of the sun, and the symbol for the Hindu religion in general.

 soybean cake.
 ik small bamboo xylophone.
 g mask or mask dance.
 angsa Bali's three high castes, the
 mana, *Satrya*, and *Wesya*,
 ditionally differentiated from the *Jaba*
 Sudra.
uak rice or palm wine.
warung food stall.

wayang kulit the two-dimensional
leather puppets or the shadow-puppet
play.

Wesya third-highest caste in the
Triwangsa, originally merchants.
Wisnu one of the holy trinity, and the
guardian of the world. known in India as
Vishnu.
wuku a period of seven days; thirty
wuku make up the 210-day Balinese year.

Yama god of the underworld.
yeh water, river, waterway.

LIST OF MAPS

INDEX